HOW TO PLAY
KEYBOARDS
ROGER EVANS

Books in the HOW TO PLAY Series

How to Play Bass Guitar
BY LAURENCE CANTY

How to Play Drums
BY JAMES BLADES AND JOHNNY DEAN

How to Play Guitar
BY ROGER EVANS

How to Play the Flute
BY HOWARD HARRISON

How to Play Keyboards
BY ROGER EVANS

How to Play Piano
BY ROGER EVANS

HOW TO PLAY
KEYBOARDS
ROGER EVANS

All you need to know
to play easy keyboard music

St. Martin's Press

NEW YORK

Library of Congress Cataloging-in-Publication Data

Evans, Roger.
How to play keyboards / Roger Evans.
p.   cm.
ISBN 0-312-08214-2
1. Electronic keyboard (Synthesizer)—Instruction and study.   I. Title.
MT192.2.E
786'193—dc20
92-9014
CIP
MN

First published in Great Britain by Elm Tree Books Ltd.

First U.S. Edition: September 1992

10 9 8 7 6 5 4 3 2 1

HOW TO PLAY
KEYBOARDS
ROGER EVANS

This book is dedicated to Mr & Mrs Floyd B. Brookens
as a special thanks for the help they gave when
an earlier book in this series was being written.

Introduction

This book is for everyone who would like to play keyboards.

Everything is explained in simple easy-to-understand stages, so you can quickly start playing good-sounding music on your keyboard. You do not need to know anything about music before you begin — simply follow the instructions and you can start playing popular tunes on your keyboard within minutes.

Electronic keyboards are the most exciting instruments today. They are so versatile they can be used to play virtually every style of music — rock, pop, classical or jazz. Modern technology puts an orchestra of sounds and rhythms at your fingertips and this book explains how you can use them to make music.

How quickly you progress is up to you. You can learn at your own speed with this book. There are no boring exercises. Instead there are entertaining tunes to play, so learning is fun right from the beginning.

All of the music in this book has been specially chosen to help you start playing quickly and easily. In every tune you will find something new, so make sure you can play each piece of music smoothly and correctly before going on.

Read one page at a time and make sure you understand everything. If necessary you can read the same page several times so you know exactly what to do. Please do not skip any pages or jump back and forth, or you may miss something important.

Your keyboard will give you a great deal of fun and enjoyment as long as you take the trouble to learn to do everything correctly right from the beginning. In music you will find the right way to play is not only the best, but also the easiest in the long run.

This book is the result of many years playing and teaching music. I hope my experience will introduce you to a lot of fun making music on your keyboard.

Roger Evans

Setting up your keyboard

Set up your keyboard where there is enough light for you to be able to read this book while you are playing.

Attach the music rest and place this book on it. If your keyboard doesn't have a music rest or if it is very flimsy, find another way of supporting the book behind the keyboard so you can read it comfortably. (A music stand, a book rest or a typists or computer copyholder are all perfect for music books.)

Find yourself a firm stool or chair. Your seat needs to be fairly high when you play, so you may need a firm cushion to put on your seat to raise it.

Sit facing your keyboard and read the first part of the instruction book which came with it. This will tell you where all the controls are, and how to work them. Point to each control as you read about it so you will know where to find it when you need it.

Check the instructions to make sure everything is connected correctly. If you are using batteries make sure they are inserted correctly. If you are using mains electricity plug in your keyboard and switch on the power.

When you are ready, switch on your keyboard, set the volume controls to a medium level and play a few notes to check everything is working properly. The first tunes in this book are played with an Organ sound, so press or slide the selector which gives an Organ 'voice'.

If at any time your keyboard does not function properly, check the instruction book to make sure you have made the right connections and set the controls correctly. If you think there is a fault, take your keyboard back to the shop where you bought it. *Never* try to repair it yourself because serious damage could result.

Helpful Hints:

Buy yourself some headphones if you haven't already got some — they need not be expensive. Then you will be able to practise and play without being overhead, even when other people are in the same room.

If your keyboard is battery powered, buy a mains adaptor if you do not already have one. An adaptor will not cost much and it will save you a lot of money for batteries.

Cover your keyboard when you are not using it to protect it from dust and dirt. Keep all drinks and liquids well away from it as any spillage could cause serious damage. You can clean the keys with a soft damp cloth — after you have switched off the keyboard. Clean the controls and facia with a soft dry cloth or feather duster.

If you carry your keyboard around, use the box it came in or a padded carry-case.

Sitting at your keyboard

Make sure your seat is high enough, so your wrists and elbows are above the level of the keyboard when you rest your fingertips on the keys. If your seat isn't high enough, find a firm cushion to sit on whenever you play.

Sit up straight facing the middle of the keyboard with your feet firmly on the ground. *Always keep your wrists up* and never let them droop. This is most important as it affects how easily and how well you will be able to play your keyboard.

Keyboard basics

Sit comfortably facing the middle of your keyboard.

Now look down at the keys. See how the black keys make a pattern — two black keys, three black keys, two black keys, three black keys, and so on:

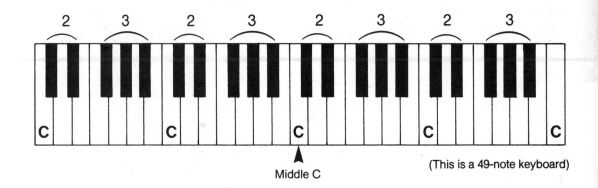

Middle C

(This is a 49-note keyboard)

The pattern of the black keys helps us find all the notes on the keyboard. The note on the left of every **two** black keys is called 'C', and the 'C' nearest the middle of the keyboard is called 'Middle C'.

Find every C on your keyboard. Then find Middle C and play it with the tip of your index finger.

The notes played on the white keys are all named after the letters of the alphabet from A to G. After G, the note names start again with A:

A   B   C   D   E   F   G   <u>A</u>   <u>B</u>   <u>C</u>   and so on

Now play Middle C and the next seven notes to the right with one finger, and say the name of each note as you play it: C   D   E   F   G   A   B   C

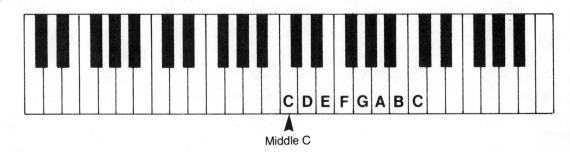

Middle C

Starting to play

Rest your right hand lightly on the keys, with your thumb on Middle C and your fingers on the next four keys:

Now draw your fingers in a little so they are slightly curved, with each fingertip resting lightly on its own key:

Remember to keep your wrist up, and play Middle C by gently pressing down with your thumb. Next lift your thumb and press down your index finger to play D. Then lift your index finger, and at the same time press down your middle finger to play E. Then relax.

Playing with a beat

Rest your right hand lightly on the keys as before, with your thumb on Middle C and your fingers on the next four keys.

Middle C

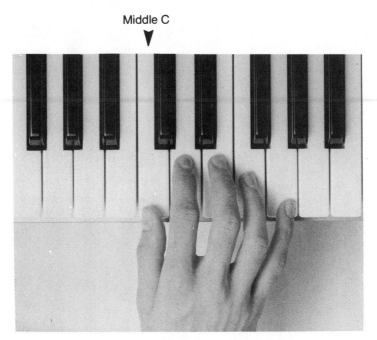

Play Middle C with your thumb, D with your index finger, and E with your middle finger several times like this:

C   D   E   D   C   D   E

Did you remember to keep your wrist up with your fingers slightly curved so you played with your fingertips? Play the notes again, then relax for a few moments.

Now press down each of your fingers *one at a time* and play C with your thumb, then D with your index finger, E with your middle finger, then F with your ring finger, then G with your little finger. Play the notes again, and try to play very smoothly. Make your fingers walk from one key to the next, so each note leads smoothly into the next note.

Let's start playing with a beat. Count *slowly* and evenly, and tap your foot as you count:

1   2   3   4 | 1   2   3   4 | 1   2   3   4 | and so on.

Keep counting slowly, and start playing in time with your counting:

1   2   3   4 | C   C   D   E | C   E   D   C | G   F   E   D | C   C   C ||

Playing your first tunes

This is how your first notes are shown in keyboard music:

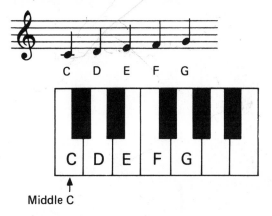

Notice how E is on the bottom line of the music 'stave', D is under the bottom line and Middle C is on an extra line under the stave. Then F is in the first space and G is on the second line of the stave. Your first tune is played with Middle C, D and E.

Rest your right-hand fingertips on the keys as before with your thumb on Middle C. Then count slowly and evenly and play each note as it occurs over the counting. Keep repeating the tune until you can play it smoothly.

MERRILY

Adapted and Arranged
by ROGER EVANS

Notes are given different shapes to tell us how long they should sound:

♩ is a QUARTER NOTE. It usually lasts for one beat.

♩ is a HALF NOTE. It usually lasts for two beats.

𝅝 is a WHOLE NOTE. It usually lasts for four beats.

Always keep the key for each note pressed down until the next note is needed, so every note lasts for its full number of beats.

The next tune is played with five notes: Middle C, D, E, F and G.

Rest your right hand lightly on the keys as before with your thumb on Middle C and your fingers on the next four keys. G is played with the little finger, and F is played with your ring finger. (If you are unsure about any of these notes go back to the previous page.) Now count evenly and play in time with your counting:

LONDON BRIDGE

Adapted and Arranged
by ROGER EVANS

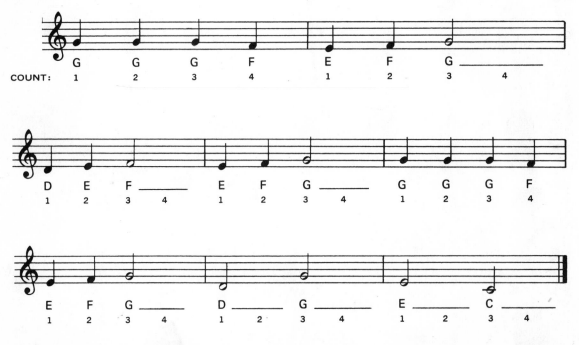

14

Exciting sounds at your fingertips

Let's begin using some of the exciting sounds which can be played on your keyboard. We started off with an Organ voice. Now let's go back and play your first tunes using different voices like Flute, Trumpet, Piano, Violin, and all of the others.

First press or slide the selector which gives a Piano voice, and play 'Merrily We Roll Along' or 'London Bridge'. Then try a different voice. Keep playing and try all of the different voices on your keyboard so you can hear how each voice sounds.

From here on in this book I will suggest voices for each tune at the beginning of the music. If you do not have the voices suggested or would like to make your own choice, choose a voice which suits the tune. The next tune sounds good with a Trumpet or Brass voice, try it. Play the same notes as before and start with your middle finger on E.

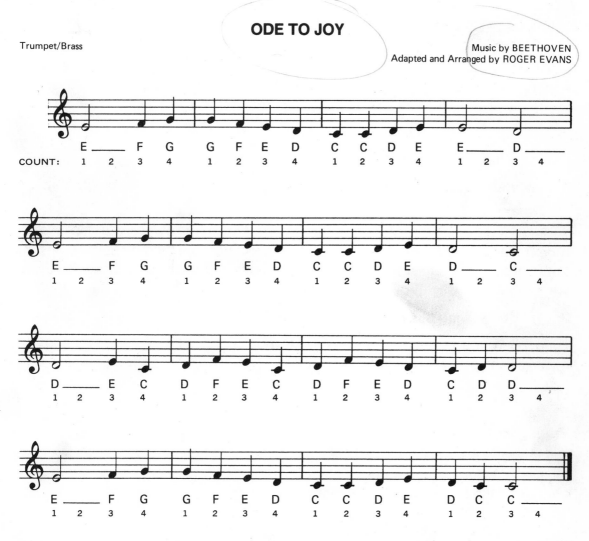

ODE TO JOY

Trumpet/Brass

Music by BEETHOVEN
Adapted and Arranged by ROGER EVANS

Practice makes perfect

The more you play the better your playing will become, and the more enjoyment you will get from your music. If you can, play a little every day or almost every day. This will help you to improve far more quickly than if you play just once or twice a week.

If possible, choose times to play when you can be on your own, or use headphones. There is nothing worse than other people listening when you are learning to play new tunes.

Start playing everything slowly. When you can play smoothly and evenly, gradually work up to the right speed. You will never play well if you try to play quickly too soon.

Try to learn something new every week, even if it is just a simple tune or learning to play with a different rhythm.

Be patient. Make sure you can play every piece of music smoothly at the right speed before going onto the next tune.

Don't be discouraged if your playing doesn't seem to improve very much from one week to the next. As long as you play regularly, keep learning new things and keep trying to improve, your playing will gradually become better all the time.

Make the most of your playing time like this:

1. Flex your fingers before you play to make them supple, and warm your hands if they are cold.

2. Practise something new, or something which you do not play very well. If part of a tune seems awkward or slows down your playing, practise this part separately for a few minutes every day until you can play it smoothly. Then try to play the whole tune smoothly all the way through.

3. Relax by playing music you already know.

Even when you are playing for fun, try to polish your playing by correcting any mistakes so you will not get into bad habits.

Playing Hint:
Try to keep your eyes on the music and play without looking down at the keys. As long as your fingers are in the right place on the keys, and you press down the correct finger each time, you will play the right notes.

The beat of the drums

The rhythm section on your keyboard is like having your own automatic drummer who will play many different rhythms for you, and change the tempo (speed) of the music at a touch of a button. The drummer's ready, let's add the beat of the drums to your music:

1. Set the rhythm: Press or slide the selector which gives a 'Ballad'. 'Pops' or 'Rock' rhythm.

2. Set the 'Tempo': Find the 'Tempo' control and set it to 'Medium' — half-way between 'fast' and 'slow'.

3. Press the 'Synchro Start' ('Synchro') button, and the rhythm is ready to play. (It will start when you press any of the keys at the left end of the keyboard.)

4. Start playing. Press any key at the left end of the keyboard with one of your left-hand fingers, and the rhythm should start.

Now, tap your foot in time with the beat and sing or hum 'London Bridge' with the rhythm. If the rhythm seems too fast or too slow, adjust the tempo control until it seems just right. If it is too loud or too soft, adjust the rhythm volume control.

5. Press 'Synchro' again or press the 'Stop' button when you want to stop the rhythm.

Playing with a drum backing

You are now ready to add a drum backing to the tunes you have been playing. I suggest you start with 'London Bridge', but you can choose whichever tune you like. If you are happier playing 'Merrily' or 'Ode To Joy', you can play either of these tunes.

1. Set the tempo control a little slower than before, and press 'Synchro'.

2. Start the rhythm by pressing any key at the left end of the keyboard with one of your left-hand fingers. (The C nearest the left end of the keyboard would be best.)

3. Rest your right hand lightly on the keys with your thumb on Middle C and listen to the rhythm. Tap your foot to the beat, hum the tune to yourself, and imagine you are playing it.

4. When you are ready, turn back to the music for the tune you have chosen and play along with your automatic drummer.

Don't stop if you make a mistake, but keep on playing with the rhythm. When you can play your first tune smoothly and confidently, start playing another tune.

Playing 'Single Finger Chords'

Attractive backings can be played on most keyboards using the 'Auto Chord' or 'Auto Bass Chord' accompaniment section. This adds chords, bass notes and drum rhythms to the tunes you play and gives your music a full and satisfying sound.

Auto chords are played by the left hand on the 'chord' keys at the left end of the keyboard. Many easy chords can be played with just one finger. Let's play some:

1. Find the selector for 'Single Finger Chords', 'Casio Chords' or 'One Finger Chords' and switch it on.

2. Rest your left hand lightly on the auto chord keys at the left end of the keyboard. Place your left thumb on the C below Middle C and your fingers on the next four keys — B, A, G and F:

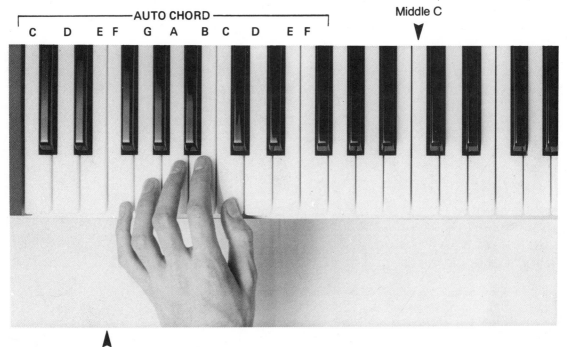

44-note keyboards end here

Now, press one key at a time and play chords:

C — Press the C key with your left thumb to play the C chord.
F — Release the C key, then press the F key with your little finger to play the F chord.
G — Release the F key, then press the G key with your ring finger to play the G chord.
C — Release the G key, then play the C chord with your thumb. Relax, then do it
   again.

Your own backing group

Add rhythm to your chords, and the music you play with your left hand will start to sound like a complete backing group! Let's try it:

1. Set the rhythm: Ballad, Pops or Rock.
2. Set the tempo: Medium.
3. Select 'Single Finger Chord', 'Casio Chord' or 'One Finger Chord'.
4. Press 'Synchro Start'.

Now your keyboard is ready to play a chord and rhythm backing. Rest your left-hand fingertips lightly on the chord keys as before, with your thumb on the C chord key, and remember to keep your wrist up.

Now follow the music, count the beat, and change chords in time with your counting. Keep the key for each chord pressed down until the next chord is needed. As you can see, the chord names — or 'Chord Symbols' as they are known — are shown over the stave in keyboard music.

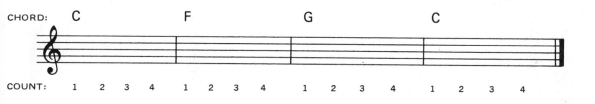

Press 'Synchro' or 'Stop' with a right-hand finger when you want to stop the rhythm. Keep repeating this 'chord sequence' until you can change chords smoothly in time with the rhythm. Then play the next slightly different sequence making sure you hold each chord for its full number of beats:

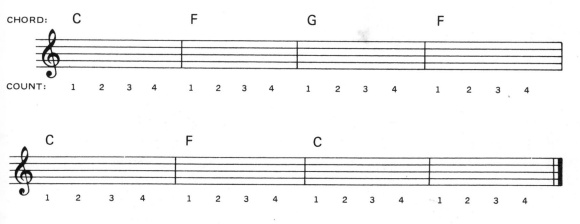

Playing melody and chords

Let's set your keyboard so you can play the next tune with both hands:

1. Set a Violin, Strings or Organ voice.
2. Set the rhythm and tempo: Ballad, Pops or Rock (Medium-Slow).
3. Select Single Finger Chord. (Or 'Casio Chord' or 'One Finger Chord'.)
4. Press Synchro Start.

Play the melody on its own first, starting with your middle finger on E. Count out loud and play in time with your counting. (Look up any notes you have forgotten on page 13.)

Next, play the chords and rhythm on their own. Then, when you are ready, press 'Synchro Start', place both hands on the keys and play melody, chords and rhythm together.

LOVE SONG

Violin/Strings or Organ
Ballad/Pops or Rock (Medium-Slow)

Music by
ROGER EVANS

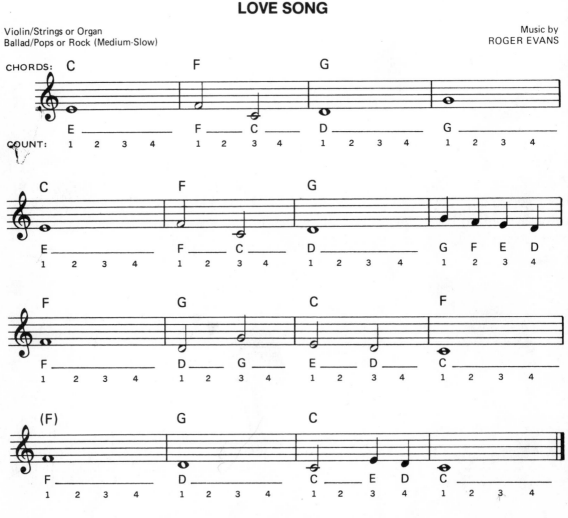

Different rhythms and voices

We'll use a different rhythm and another voice for the next tune. All keyboards do not have the same rhythms or voices, so I will give a choice. If you have both voices or rhythms, try them both and make your own choice. Let's set the keyboard ready to play:

1. Select one of the voices suggested at the beginning of the tune: Vibes or Piano.
2. Set one of the rhythms, and the tempo: March or Rock (Medium).
3. Select Single Finger Chord.   4. Press Synchro Start.

'Jingle Bells' is played with the same 5 notes and 3 chords which you have been playing, so rest both hands lightly on the keys in the same places as before.
Play the melody on its own, then the chords and rhythm. Then set the tempo a little slower for the first few times, press 'Synchro Start' and play with both hands together.

JINGLE BELLS

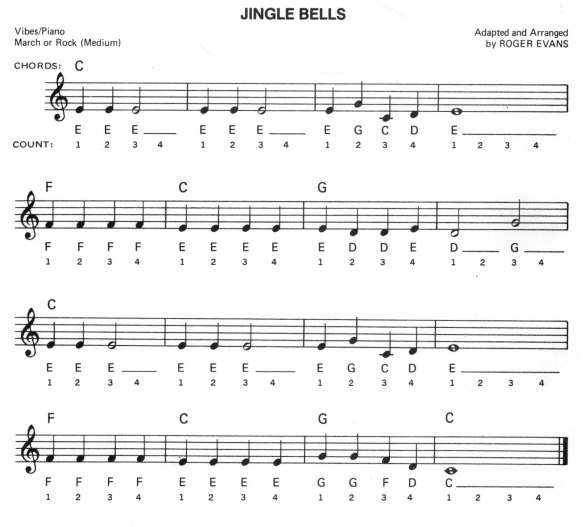

Vibes/Piano
March or Rock (Medium)

Adapted and Arranged
by ROGER EVANS

More about music

At the beginning of music you will usually see two numbers or a sign. These tell us how many beats there are in the rhythm of the music.

If the top number is '3', the music has a 3-beat rhythm:

    is counted   1   2   3 | 1   2   3 | and so on.

If the top number is '4', or there is a sign like a large 'C', the music has a 4-beat rhythm:

    or   is counted   1   2   3   4 | 1   2   3   4 | and so on.

You will often find one note joined to the next note with a curved line called a 'tie'. Think of this as one long note which lasts for the same number of beats as the notes which are joined:

COUNT: 1   2   3   4   1   2   3   4
MAKE THE NOTE LAST THIS LONG

Notes are also made longer when they have a small dot after them. The dot makes the note half as long again:

♩ lasts two beats, so ♩. should last three beats.

The next tune is played with a three-beat rhythm. It also has some 'tied' notes and 'dotted' notes for you to play.

A classic waltz

As you can see, the next tune has a three-beat rhythm. This means you should count slowly: <u>1</u> 2 3 <u>1</u> 2 3 to work out the timing of the melody. It also means we will use a 'Waltz' rhythm, because three-beat tunes are usually waltzes.

Set the rhythm and one of the voices suggested at the beginning of the tune. If you like, you can use 'variation' or 'arpeggio', if your keyboard has one of these effects, but remember to switch it off again when you finish playing.

Follow the counting and play the melody on its own. (You can look up any notes you have forgotten on page 13.) Then, when you are ready, press 'Synchro Start' and play the melody and chords together.

BARCAROLLE

Violin/Strings
Waltz (Medium) (Add Variation/Arpeggio)

Music by JACQUES OFFENBACH
Adapted and Arranged by ROGER EVANS

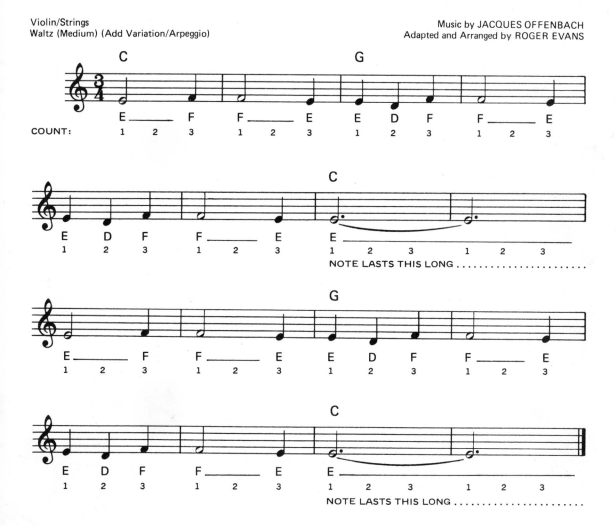

A song from the Caribbean

This easy version of Mary-Ann is played with the same five notes and three chords as the other tunes you have been playing.

This traditional song from the Caribbean sounds good with a 'Bossa Nova' rhythm, so set this rhythm and choose one of the voices suggested at the beginning of the music. Also set the tempo: Medium-Fast (a little faster than before). Now press 'Synchro Start' and play chords and rhythm on their own to get the feeling of the Bossa Nova beat.

Next, follow the counting and play the melody on its own. Remember to make the 'tied' notes last for their full number of beats. When you are ready, press 'Synchro Start' again and play with both hands together.

MARY-ANN

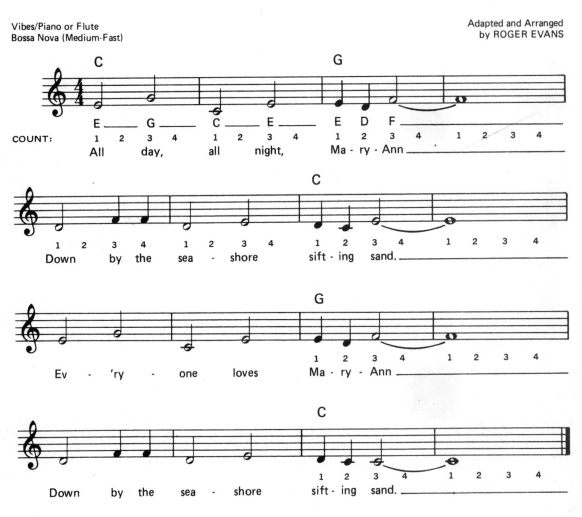

A jazz tune to play

The next tune is played with the 'Swing' rhythm, which is used for many jazz tunes. Set the rhythm and tempo: Swing (Medium-Fast). Then choose one of the voices suggested at the beginning of the music: Trumpet, Brass, Jazz Organ or Organ 2.

Play the melody on its own first.   This tune starts on the second beat, so count: 1 2 3 4 and start playing as you count '2'.

The chords come in after the melody at the beginning of the tune, but this is no problem. Simply press 'Synchro Start' before you begin and follow the music. If you don't get the beginning right first time, stop the rhythm, press 'Synchro' once more and try it again.

WHEN THE SAINTS GO MARCHING IN

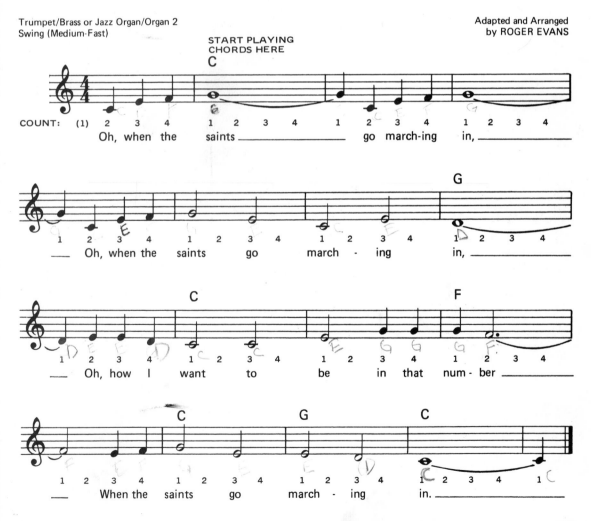

More notes to play

Move your right hand three keys to the right from where you have been playing, and your fingers will be in position to play three new notes— A, B and another C.

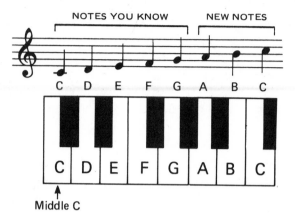

Notice how these 'new' notes appear in music —
A is in the second space; B is on the middle line and C is in the third space.

Also notice how the 'stems' of notes can go up (♩) or down (♩) — it makes no difference to the notes.

Now rest your right-hand fingertips lightly on the keys, with your thumb on **F** and your fingers on the next four white keys — **G, A, B** and **C:**

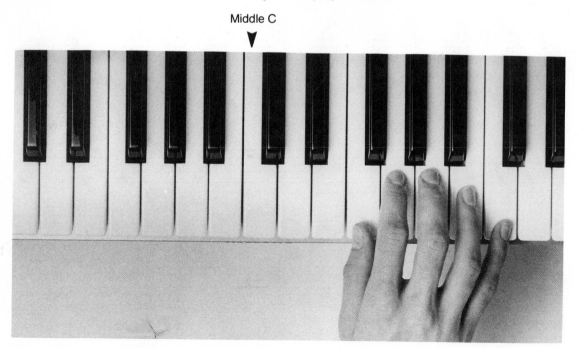

Play these notes one at a time and say the name of each note as you play it: Play F with your thumb, then G with your index finger, then A with your middle finger, then B with your ring finger, then C with your little finger:

Keep playing these notes and saying their names. Then follow the counting and play this short piece of music with these notes — it's the first part of a famous song. Start with your little finger on C, and start playing on the second beat — as you count '2'.

If you like, you can add chords and rhythm when you know how to play the melody.

O SOLE MIO

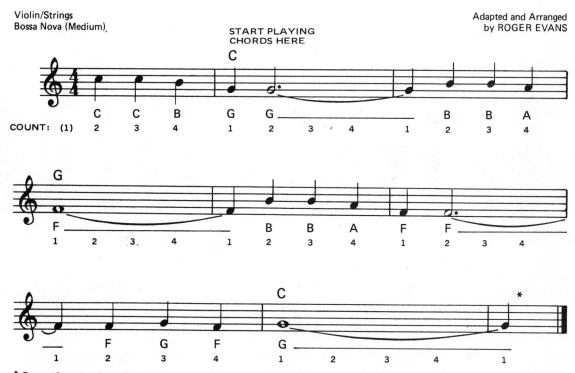

* Press 'Synchro' or 'Stop' here with a right-hand finger to stop the rhythm.

Fingering

Your thumbs and fingers are given numbers to tell you which fingers to use when you play notes in different places on the keyboard. The thumb is '1', the index finger '2', the middle finger '3', and so on:

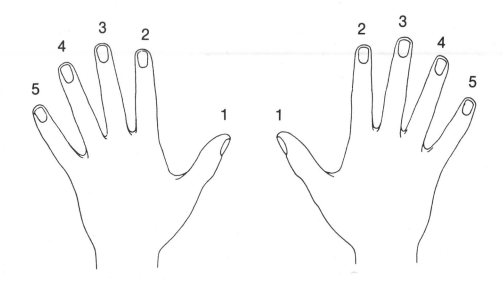

'Fingering' can be really helpful because it guides your fingers from one note to the next note when you move around the keyboard.

In the next piece of music, the '1' in front of the first note suggests you play this note with your thumb. Then you spread your fingers to play E with your index finger (2), then G with your middle finger (3), the higher C with your little finger (5), and so on. Follow the fingering and play this:

Finger numbers are marked in front of notes in this book where the fingering is not obvious or where your hand needs to move to a different place on the keys.

If finger numbers are not marked for part of a tune it means your hand should stay in the same place with your fingers next to each other on the keys.

In the next tune the right hand starts in one place on the keys, moves to another place and plays there for a while; then moves back again to play where it started.

Play the melody on its own first. Start with your thumb on Middle C, follow the fingering carefully, and make sure you play the right notes with the right fingers. As you can see the fingering is given all the way through this tune.

'On Top Of Old Smoky' is played with a waltz rhythm. The tune begins on the 3rd beat, so count 1   2   3 and start playing as you count '3'.

(If you are unsure of any of the notes, you can look them up on page 26.)

ON TOP OF OLD SMOKY

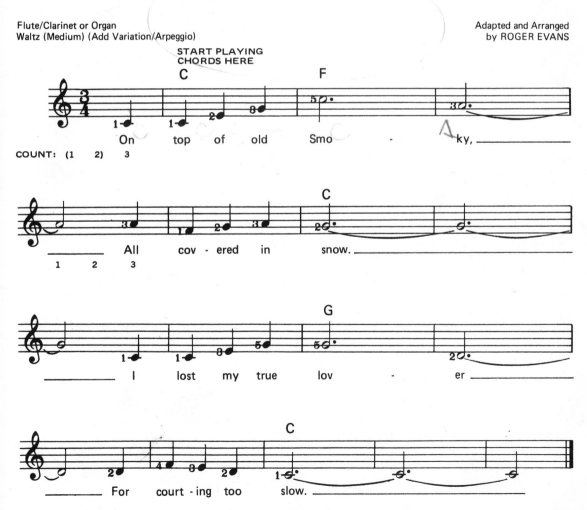

Flute/Clarinet or Organ
Waltz (Medium) (Add Variation/Arpeggio)

Adapted and Arranged
by ROGER EVANS

29

Playing runs of notes

You can play smooth runs of notes towards the right of the keyboard by passing your thumb under your fingers like this:

Try this: Play Middle C with your right thumb (1), then D with your index finger (2), then play E with your middle finger (3). *Keep your middle finger on E, bring your thumb under your fingers and play F with your thumb:*

Your wrist should stay straight and not twist when your thumb moves under your fingers.

Now follow the fingering and play all of the notes shown here. This is called a 'Scale of C':

SCALE OF C

Flute/Clarinet

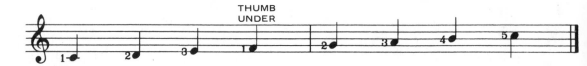

You can play smooth runs of notes towards the *left* of the keyboard by bringing your middle finger — or another finger — over your thumb, like this:

Try this: Play A with your middle finger (3), then play G with your index finger (2), then play F with your thumb (1). *Keep your thumb on F; bring your middle finger over your thumb, and play E with your middle finger.* Then play D with your index finger, then play Middle C with your thumb:

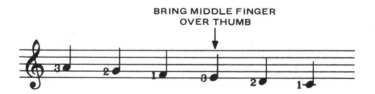

Play the next piece of music several times until you can play it smoothly. Start slowly at first, then speed up when you can play evenly. Use this 'scale' to warm-up your fingers whenever you play. It will help you to learn to play smooth runs of notes up and down the keyboard.

SCALE OF C — UP AND DOWN

Trumpet/Brass

Eighth notes

In many tunes you will find notes which last for less than one beat.

♪ is an EIGHTH NOTE. It usually lasts for half a beat.

Eighth notes are often joined to other eighth notes, like this:

TWO
EIGHTH NOTES

FOUR
EIGHTH NOTES

Tap your foot and count eighth notes by saying 'and' between each beat:

COUNT: 1   and   2   and   3   and   4   and

You will often find eighth notes with 'dotted' quarter notes. (Remember, a dot after a note makes it last half as long again!):

♩ lasts for one beat, so ♩. must last for one and a half beats.

You can count dotted quarter notes and eighth notes like this:

COUNT: 1   2   and   3   4   and

Count the beat and play this little example with one finger on any note, so you will know how to play the dotted quarter notes and eighth notes in the next tune.

A song to sing

Play the melody on its own at first. Follow the fingering carefully, count the beat slowly and play in time with your counting.

When you are ready, set your keyboard for one of the voices and rhythms suggested at the beginning of the tune, press Synchro Start, and play the melody along with the chords and rhythm.

You can sing along with your keyboard, like this:

Play the tune once. Don't stop when you come to the end, but keep playing the last chord. Then, give your right hand a rest and sing along while your left hand plays the chords again from the beginning.

MICHAEL ROW THE BOAT ASHORE

Jazz Organ/Organ 2 or Flute
Bossa Nova or Ballad/Pops/Rock (Medium)

Adapted and Arranged
by ROGER EVANS

2. Sister, help to trim the sail, Hallelujah.
   Sister, help to trim the sail, Hallelujah.

3. Jordan's River is deep and wide, Hallelujah.
   Meet my friends on the other side, Hallelujah.

4. Repeat first verse.

More tunes to play

The next two tunes will help you to practise what you have learned so far.

The first tune is a traditional song from the sunny Caribbean. You can play it with the Samba rhythm, and it makes a good dance tune.

Follow the counting (and fingering) and play the melody on its own at first. Then add the chords and rhythm. If you like you can keep counting and playing chords at the end and play the tune through again, or sing along with your playing.

BROWN GIRL IN THE RING

Electric Guitar/Piano or Jazz Organ
Samba (Medium)

Adapted and Arranged
by ROGER EVANS

The next tune is a famous classical melody.

You can use 'variation' or 'arpeggio' to fill out the backing if your keyboard has either of these effects. This usually sounds good with the waltz rhythm.

BRAHMS' LULLABY

Piano or Violin
Waltz (Slow) (Add Variation/Arpeggio)

Adapted and Arranged
by ROGER EVANS

High notes and low notes

We are now going to play some notes at top of the stave — as well as some notes written under the stave.

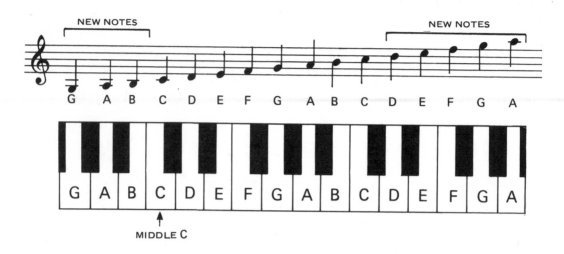

Let's start with the low notes. Play Middle C with your ring finger (4), then B with your middle finger (3), then A with your index finger (2), then G with your thumb (1):

Now play the high notes, starting with your thumb on D:

Rests: In many tunes the melody or accompaniment 'takes a rest' and is silent for a few beats. These silent beats are called 'rests', and they are shown in music like this:

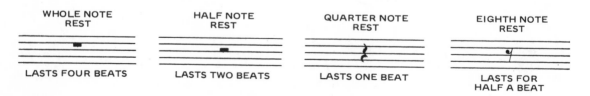

The next tune starts low down on the keyboard with your right thumb playing the G below Middle C. Then your right hand moves up the keyboard to play the notes at the top of the stave. (If you are unsure of any of the notes you can look them up on the opposite page.)

This tune has a new chord — 'D'. Play D by moving your left thumb one key to the right when you come to this chord; then play the next C chord with your index finger.

Play the melody on its own before you add the chords. Then play the tune through twice.

ONE DAY IN MY LIFE

Piano
Waltz (Medium-Slow) (Add Variation/Arpeggio)

Music by
ROGER EVANS

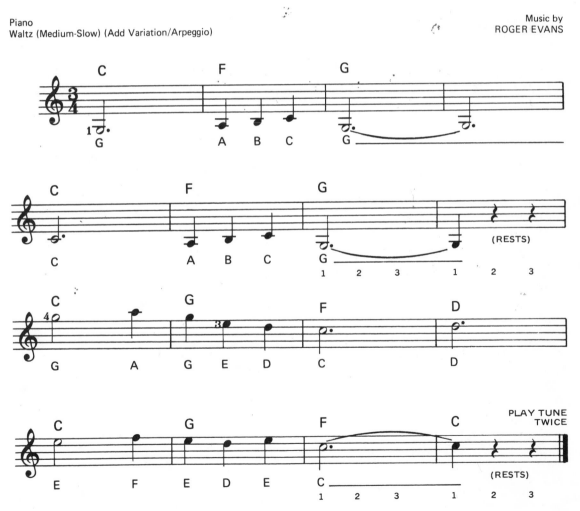

A famous Irish song

'O Danny Boy' is played with some of the new notes introduced on the previous pages.

It is longer than the tunes which you have played so far, but you can learn to play it in two parts if you like:

Start by learning to play the first part of the tune, and follow the fingering carefully. (The first part ends at the top of the next page.) Then learn to play the second part of the tune before you put it all together. (If you are unsure of any of the notes look them up on page 36.)

Notice how the chords start one beat before the melody in this tune:

O DANNY BOY

Organ or Flute
Ballad/Pops (Medium-Slow) (Add Variation/Arpeggio)

Adapted and Arranged
by ROGER EVANS

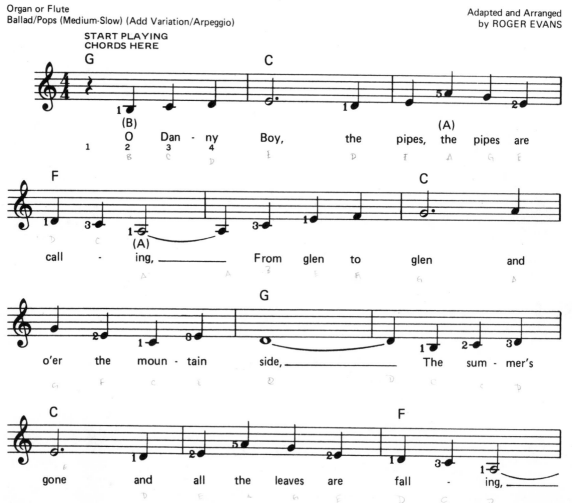

SECOND PART OF TUNE

It's you, it's you must go, and I must bide.

(G) (A) (B) (C) (B)
But hur - ry back when sum - mer's in the

(G) (A) (B) (C)
mea - dow, Or when the val - ley's

hushed and white with snow. Then I'll be

(E) (D) (D) (C) (A)
here in sun - shine and in sha - dow,

(B)
O Dan - ny Boy, O Dan - ny Boy, I love you

(A) (B)

so.

1 2 3 4 1

* Stop rhythm here

39

Playing minor chords

There is another important set of chords which can be played automatically on most keyboards. These chords are called 'minor chords', and they are shown in music with a small 'm' after the chord name: 'Cm' means 'C minor'.

Set your keyboard for 'single finger chords', and you can play minor chords by pressing two keys at the same time with two left-hand fingers.

The keys which you press to play minor chords vary for different makes of keyboards, so look in your instruction manual to find out how you play minor chords on your instrument. Then tick the method here which applies to your keyboard:

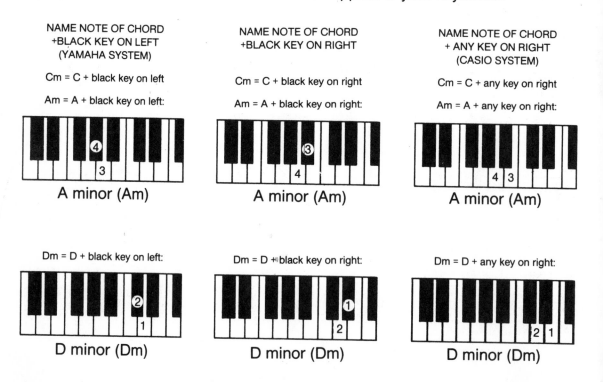

NAME NOTE OF CHORD
+BLACK KEY ON LEFT
(YAMAHA SYSTEM)

Cm = C + black key on left

Am = A + black key on left:

A minor (Am)

Dm = D + black key on left:

D minor (Dm)

NAME NOTE OF CHORD
+BLACK KEY ON RIGHT

Cm = C + black key on right

Am = A + black key on right:

A minor (Am)

Dm = D + black key on right:

D minor (Dm)

NAME NOTE OF CHORD
+ ANY KEY ON RIGHT
(CASIO SYSTEM)

Cm = C + any key on right

Am = A + any key on right:

A minor (Am)

Dm = D + any key on right:

D minor (Dm)

Set your keyboard for 'single finger chords', and play these chords with the left-hand fingering given here for your type of keyboard.

IMPORTANT: Always make sure you press and release both keys at *exactly the same time* when you play minor chords, or the wrong chord may sound.

Now play this chord sequence. Start with your left index finger (2) on the C chord key:

Slow Rock (Medium)

| C | Am | Dm | G | C | |

A tune with minor chords

This famous Spanish melody is a favourite guitar solo.

Play the melody and chords separately at first, before you play with both hands together. Play the Am and Dm chords with the fingering you used on the facing page; play the C chord with your middle finger, and play the E chord with your thumb.

SPANISH ROMANCE

Guitar/Piano
Waltz (Medium-Slow) (Add Variation/Arpeggio)

Adapted and Arranged
by ROGER EVANS

* Stop the rhythm by pressing 'Synchro' or 'Stop' with a right-hand finger just after you count '1'.

More tunes with minor chords

This traditional Gaelic melody was given new words to become 'Morning Has Broken'.

Start with your left thumb on the C chord key, and play the F chord with your little finger; the D chord with your thumb, and the G chord with your ring finger (4). Play the Am chord with your middle finger (3) and ring finger (4) as before.

MORNING

Flute or Organ
Waltz (Medium-Slow) (Add Variation/Arpeggio)

Adapted and Arranged
by ROGER EVANS

* Stop the rhythm by pressing 'Synchro' or 'Stop' just after you count '1'.

'House Of The Rising Sun' has a six-beat rhythm and is played with a 'Slow Rock' backing. This gives it a very different feeling to other tunes you have played.

Play the Am chord with the same fingering as before. Play chords and rhythm only for the first time through. Then play the melody with the chords.

HOUSE OF THE RISING SUN

Organ
Slow Rock (Medium-Slow) (Add Variation/Arpeggio)

Adapted and Arranged
by ROGER EVANS

* Second time through, press 'Synchro' or 'Stop' here to stop the rhythm.

43

Special effects

You are already using some of the most important effects on your keyboard, and by now you probably can't imagine playing without 'Synchro Start', automatic bass, chords and rhythms and 'variation' or 'arpeggio'. On most modern keyboards you will find some other effects, and we will be using a few more of them from now on. (If your keyboard doesn't have all of these effects, do not worry — they are not essential.)

Duet. (This is called **Counter Melody** or **Auto Harmonize** on some keyboards.) Duet adds an automatic harmony and sounds like two instruments playing together. It can work very well, especially if used for part of a tune, but don't over-use it.

Stereo Chorus or **Symphonic Chorus** gives a full stereo sound. If you have either of these effects try using them with Organ, Piano, Flute, Violin and other voices.

Intro/Ending and **Fill-In** are like automatic drum solos which can be played at the beginning, ending and even in the middle of tunes. Try this with Mary-Ann and a few other tunes: Press the Intro/Ending or Fill-in button, then press the chord key for the first chord of the tune. You should hear a drum solo for four or eight beats. Tap your foot to the rhythm, and start playing the melody when the drum solo stops.

You can also use the Intro/Ending effect to finish a tune — simply press the button when you have played the last note of the melody. If you do not have an Intro/Ending feature of your keyboard, you can finish most tunes in the same way we've been finishing 3-beat tunes — by counting 1-2-3-1 and pressing 'Synchro' or 'Stop' just after you count the last '1'. You can finish 4-beat tunes in the same way by counting 1-2-3-4-1, and pressing 'Synchro' or 'Stop' just after you count the last '1'.

Another minor chord — E minor

Here is another minor chord to play with 'single finger chords'. Use the same method as before for minor chords, and follow the fingering for your type of keyboard. (Go back to page 40, or look in your instruction manual if you are unsure what to do.)

NAME NOTE OF CHORD +BLACK KEY ON LEFT (YAMAHA SYSTEM)	NAME NOTE OF CHORD +BLACK KEY ON RIGHT	NAME NOTE OF CHORD + ANY KEY ON RIGHT (CASIO SYSTEM)
Em = E + black key on left:	Em = E + black key on right:	Em = E + any key on right:
E minor (Em)	E minor (Em)	E minor (Em)

Pachelbel's Canon is a very popular classical piece which has featured in several major films. This music can be a real 'show-stopper' if you add a few special effects.

Practise the chords on their own, then add the melody. If you like, you could play the tune once, then add Duet and play the music again from the beginning.

PACHELBEL'S CANON

Violin or Flute (Add Stereo Chorus or Stereo Symphonic)
Ballad/Pops (Medium-Slow) (Add Variation/Arpeggio)
(Add Duet)

Adapted and Arranged
by ROGER EVANS

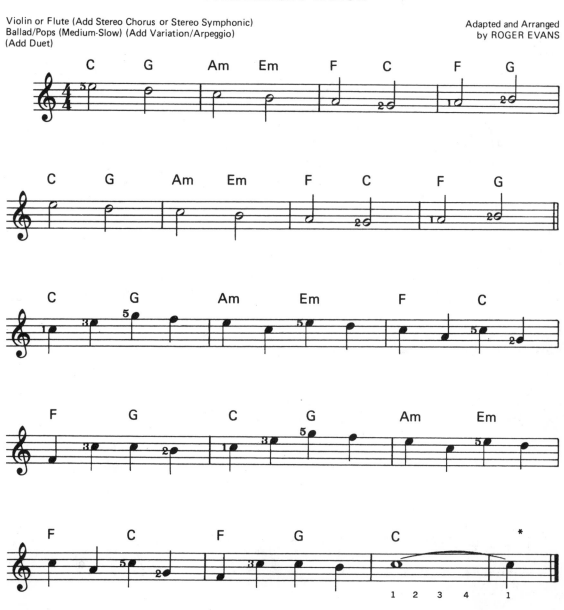

Playing notes on the black keys

The notes played on the black keys are called 'Sharps' (♯) and 'Flats' (♭).

Sharp notes are played on the keys to the right of the 'natural' notes with the same letter names:

C sharp (C♯) is played on the black key to the right of C.
F sharp (F♯) is played on the black key to the right of F,
and so on:

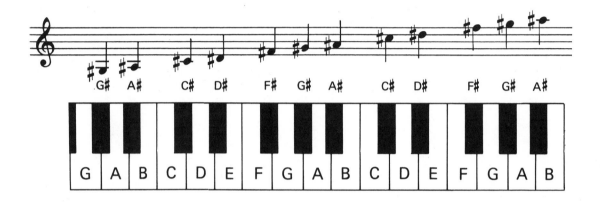

Play all of the notes on the black keys, and say the name of each note out loud as you play it: G♯ (G sharp); A♯ (A sharp); C♯ (C sharp); D♯ (D sharp); F♯ (F sharp) and so on.

Here, the sharp sign (♯) in front of the note C means you should play C♯ (on the black key) instead of C. Play this:

This famous American song includes a C sharp (C♯) for you to play. Follow the fingering carefully, as the melody moves around the keyboard.

AMERICA THE BEAUTIFUL

Organ or Flute
Ballad/Pops (Medium) (Add Variation/Arpeggio)

Adapted and Arranged
by ROGER EVANS

Key signatures

Sharp signs (♯) or flat signs (♭) at the beginning of every line of music are called 'key signatures'. The key signature with one sharp has the ♯ sign on the F line of the stave. This means you should play F♯ instead of *every F, all through the music:*

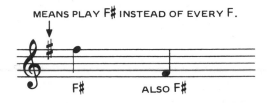

MEANS PLAY F♯ INSTEAD OF EVERY F.

F♯   ALSO F♯

Here are the notes you can expect to find in music with one sharp in the key signature. Remember that F♯ must be played instead of *every F*, even though there are no sharp signs in front of the notes:

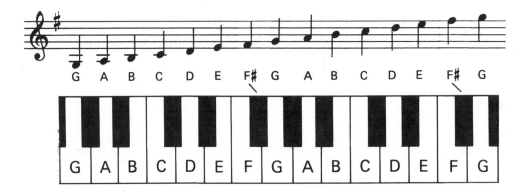

Playing Hint:
Before you play a new tune for the first time, look through the music to make sure you know how to play all of the notes and chords. Look up any notes or chords you have forgotten, so you won't need to stop playing in the middle of the music.

Play the melody on its own first to work out the fingering. Then run through the chords so you know how to change smoothly from one chord to the next. Always make sure you can play the melody and chords smoothly before you play with both hands together.

A blues song

This favourite jazz and blues song has F♯ in the key signature, so play F♯ instead of every F all through the music. (All of the other notes are played on the white keys.)

Play single finger chords starting with your little finger on the G chord key, and your thumb on the D chord key. Play the E chord by moving your thumb one key to the right; play the A chord with your ring finger (4) and the C chord with your index finger (2).

This tune can be played with the jazzy Swing rhythm or as a Slow Rock. Why not try it both ways? If you like, you could start this tune with a drum break. Simply press the Intro/Ending or Fill-in button, then press the G chord key just before you begin.

CARELESS LOVE

Jazz Organ/Organ 2
Swing or Slow Rock (Medium)

Adapted and Arranged
by ROGER EVANS

49

More tunes to play with sharps

The next piece of music was written by one of the most famous classical composers of all time — Johann Sebastian Bach.

One sharp (♯) in the key signature means you should play F♯ instead of every F. Follow the fingering carefully so your fingers 'walk' smoothly from one note to the next.

MINUET FOR LOVERS

Harpsichord/Piano or Flute
Waltz (Medium-Slow) (Add Variation/Arpeggio)

Music by JOHANN SEBASTIAN BACH
Adapted and Arranged by ROGER EVANS

This beautiful English song has become a popular music standard.

Make sure you can change chords smoothly, and play the melody easily before you play with both hands together. Play the E minor chord with the fingering you used on page 44. Play the D chord with your middle finger (3). Play the B chord with your little finger (5) on the B chord key.

SCARBOROUGH FAIR

Flute or Organ
Waltz (Medium-Slow) (Add Variation/Arpeggio)

Adapted and Arranged
by ROGER EVANS

Flats

Flat notes are played on the keys *to the left* of the 'natural' notes with the same letter names:

A flat (A♭) is played on the black key to the left of A.
B flat (B♭) is played on the black key to the left of B.
E flat (E♭) is played on the black key to the left of E,
and so on.

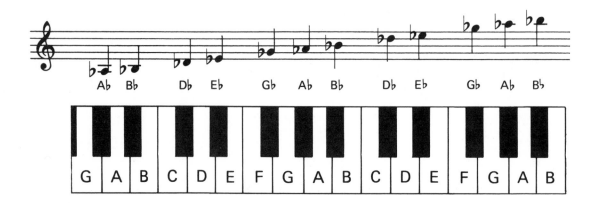

All of the notes played on the black keys can have a sharp name or a flat name. On the keyboard C sharp (C♯) is the same as D flat (D♭), and so on.

Play all of the notes on the black keys, and say the name of each note out loud as you play it: A♭ (A flat); B♭ (B flat); D♭ (D flat); E♭ (E flat); G♭ (G flat), and so on.

Here, the flat sign (♭) in front of the note B means you should play B♭ (on the black key), instead of B. Play this:

Your next piece of music is a famous melody by Frederic Chopin.

This classical theme includes a B♭ note (B flat) for you to play. Play the melody on its own at first and follow the fingering carefully. Then add the chords and rhythm.

FANTASIE

Piano or Violin/Strings
Ballad/Pops (Medium-Slow) (Add Variation/Arpeggio)

Music by FREDERIC CHOPIN
Adapted and Arranged by ROGER EVANS

Flat key signatures

The key signature with one flat has the ♭ sign in the position of the note B at the beginning of every line of music. This means you should play B♭ instead of *every* B, all through the music:

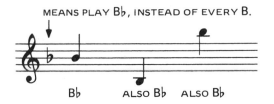

MEANS PLAY B♭, INSTEAD OF EVERY B.

B♭   ALSO B♭   ALSO B♭

Here are the notes you can expect to find in music with one flat in the key signature. Remember that B♭ must be played instead of *every* B, even though there are no ♭ signs in front of the notes:

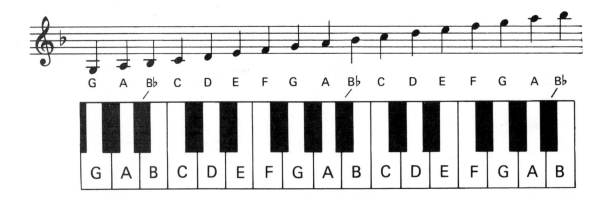

Natural Signs (♮): A 'natural sign' (♮) in front of a note means you should play the natural note (on the white key) instead of a sharp or flat which was marked earlier.

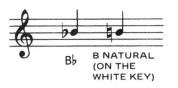

B♭   B NATURAL
(ON THE
WHITE KEY)

F♯   F NATURAL
(ON THE
WHITE KEY)

'Love Sweet Love' is a version of the French song 'Plaisir D'Amour'. Here it has one flat in the key signature, so play B♭ instead of every B, all through the music.

Play the B♭ chord with your left index finger (2) on the black key to the left of the B chord key. Play the F chord with your little finger, and the C chord with your thumb.

Keep playing chords when you come to the end of the music. Then press 'Duet' with a right-hand finger and play the tune again.

LOVE SWEET LOVE

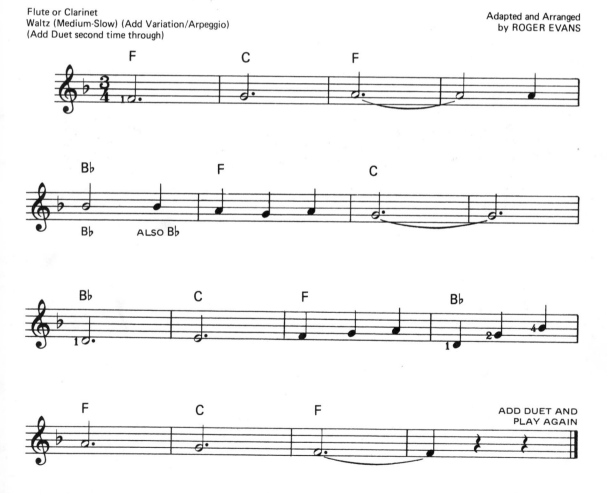

Flute or Clarinet
Waltz (Medium-Slow) (Add Variation/Arpeggio)
(Add Duet second time through)

Adapted and Arranged
by ROGER EVANS

More tunes to play with flats

This beautiful melody from the American Civil War has become a modern popular song.

Once again, the music has B♭ in the key signature so remember to play B♭ instead of B. Also remember to play the B♭ chord on the black B♭ chord key. Notice how the last line is played an extra time, to give the song a neat ending.

AURA LEE

Violin/Strings
Slow Rock (Medium)

Adapted and Arranged
by ROGER EVANS

* The tune really finishes here, but we'll play the last line again to make a neat ending.

This great song from Wales has B♭ in the key signature, so play B♭ instead of B.

Watch out for the fingering, because your right-hand fingers need to change places on the keys to play some of the notes.

ALL THROUGH THE NIGHT

Trombone/Trumpet or Brass
Ballad/Pops or Rock (Medium)

Adapted and Arranged
by ROGER EVANS

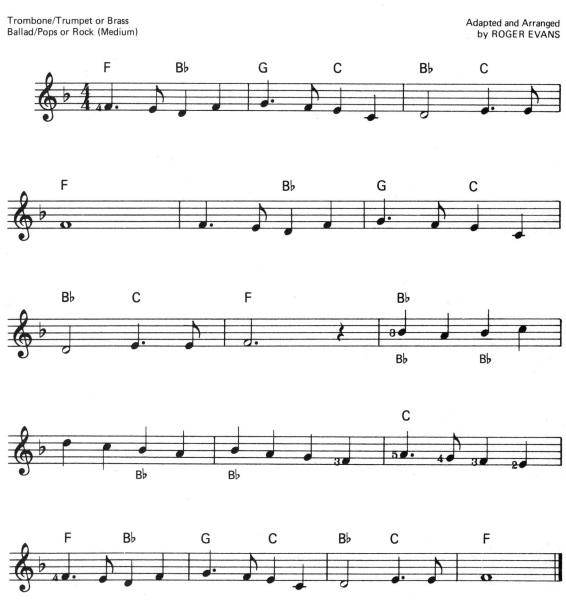

Playing seventh chords

Another important set of chords called 'seventh' chords' can be played automatically on most keyboards. Seventh chords are shown in keyboard music with a '7' after the chord name — 'C7' means 'C seventh'.

Seventh chords are played in various ways on different makes of keyboards. Look in your instruction manual to find out which keys you press to play seventh chords in the 'single finger chord' mode on your instrument. Then tick the method here which applies to your keyboard. Always press all keys down at exactly the same time:

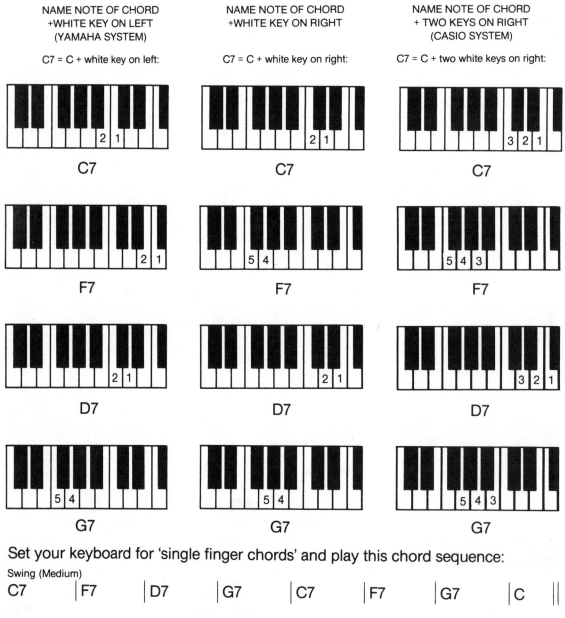

NAME NOTE OF CHORD
+WHITE KEY ON LEFT
(YAMAHA SYSTEM)

C7 = C + white key on left:

NAME NOTE OF CHORD
+WHITE KEY ON RIGHT

C7 = C + white key on right:

NAME NOTE OF CHORD
+ TWO KEYS ON RIGHT
(CASIO SYSTEM)

C7 = C + two white keys on right:

C7   C7   C7

F7   F7   F7

D7   D7   D7

G7   G7   G7

Set your keyboard for 'single finger chords' and play this chord sequence:

Swing (Medium)

C7 | F7 | D7 | G7 | C7 | F7 | G7 | C ||

There are also 'minor seventh' chords which can be played automatically on many keyboards. Minor sevenths are marked 'm7' in keyboard music — 'Cm7' means 'C minor seventh'. Look in your instruction manual to see how they are played on your keyboard.

It is not always essential to play seventh chords, and for this reason they are often shown in brackets in easy keyboard music. G(7) means you can play a G7 chord or a G chord. Cm(7) means you can play either Cm7 or Cm.

This easy little tune lets you hear how seventh chords work. Play it both ways, with and without the seventh chords, and hear how much fuller it sounds with seventh chords:

BANKS OF THE OHIO

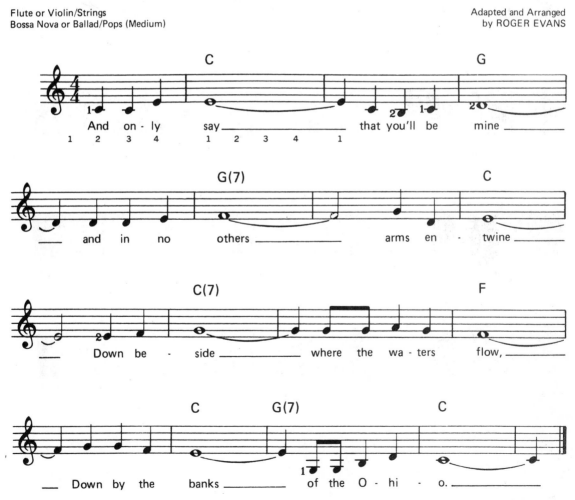

Flute or Violin/Strings
Bossa Nova or Ballad/Pops (Medium)

Adapted and Arranged
by ROGER EVANS

A song for Christmas...

This popular Christmas song makes an excellent keyboard solo. Play it once, keep playing chords while you select 'Duet', then play the tune again.

The seventh chords are not essential for this tune, so you can play G7 or G chords — try it both ways. (As you can see, there are no sharps or flats in this music.)

SILENT NIGHT

Organ/Pipe Organ
Waltz (Medium-Slow) (Add Variation/Arpeggio)
(Add Duet second time through)

Adapted and Arranged
by ROGER EVANS

* Select Duet, Counter Melody or Auto Harmonize and play the tune again.

Read music as often as possible

The more you read music, the easier it becomes, so practise reading music whenever you can. Look for new music to read — it doesn't have to be keyboard music. Anything with the 𝄞 clef and chord symbols will do as long as it isn't too complicated. Look for books of music in your local music shop or library.

Choose simple music at first — tunes which are not too long, without too many sharps or flats in the key signature. If you are buying music, see the advice given on page 86. Every new tune will help you to read music more quickly and play better.

Learn from other musicians

Listen to keyboard music as often as you can — on records and on radio and TV. Listen closely to all types of music and different styles of playing, and try to imagine how you would play them.

Go out and watch other musicians playing, preferably in places where you can get close enough to watch what the keyboard player is doing. The players do not have to be 'big-name' performers. You can learn from anyone who plays in public as long as you remember the basic rules and do not pick up another musician's bad habits.

Do not be put off by the high standard of playing by musicians you see. Remember they were once beginners who have gone through all the steps you are taking.

Do you need lessons?

If you are happy with what you play, you can probably manage without taking lessons as long as you play enough different music and learn from other musicians. However, lessons are almost essential if you take your keyboard playing seriously.

Lessons can really improve your playing. A good teacher will help you to progress far more quickly than you could on your own. He or she will suggest suitable music for you to play, explain how different techniques are played and help you in many other ways.

If you want to take lessons, choose a teacher who is expert in the sort of music you want to play. Your local music shop or keyboard dealer may be able to recommend someone and give you an idea of the cost of lessons. Otherwise look for advertisements in keyboard magazines. Talk to the teacher about your standard of playing and the sort of music you want to play before you commit yourself to a series of lessons. Also decide whether you want individual lessons or lessons in a group or class.

Very important: Get the most out of your lessons by practising what the teacher suggests.

Repeat signs

'Repeat signs' are often used where part of the music is to be played more than once:

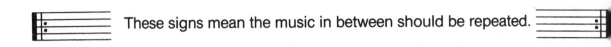 These signs mean the music in between should be repeated.

FIRST and SECOND TIME SIGNS:

First time through play the music marked 1.

Second time around play the music marked 2. instead.

D.C. — means repeat the music from the beginning.

D.S. ‰ — means go back and repeat the music from this sign: ‰

D.‰. al Coda — means go back to the sign ‰ and repeat the music until you see *To Coda* ⊕ Then play the music marked ⊕ *CODA*

D.‰ al Fine — means go back to the sign ‰ and repeat the music until you come to the word *Fine* (Finish).

D.C. al Fine — means return to the beginning and repeat the music until you come to the word *Fine* (Finish).

You can come back to this page and look up these signs whenever you find them in music.

How To Read Music, also written by Roger Evans, explains all of the musical signs, notes and musical words which you are ever likely to find in music.

This popular fisherman's song from the Bahamas has been a hit several times.

Follow the repeat signs and play the music marked  1. the first time through, then leave it out and play the music marked 2. instead on the second time around.

SLOOP JOHN B

Trumpet/Brass or Vibes
Bossa Nova (Medium)

Adapted and Arranged
by ROGER EVANS

We came on the Sloop John B, My old grand dad-dy and me,
hoist up the John B sails See how the main sail's set,

All a - round Nas - sau Town We did roam. ___ Drink - ing all
Send for the captain a - shore Let me go home, ___ Let me go

night ___ Got in a fight, ___
home ___ Let me go home, ___

feel so broke up, I want to go home. *Chorus:* So
feel so broke up, I want to go home.

I feel so broke up, I want to go home. ___

65

This beautiful South American flute tune provided the haunting melody for a hit song for Paul Simon.

Here it shows how repeat signs work in popular music. Simply follow the instructions as you play the music, and you will see  and Coda signs in action.

EL CONDOR PASA

Flute (Add Stereo Chorus/Stereo Symphonic)
March (Medium)

Adapted and Arranged
by ROGER EVANS

SECOND TIME THROUGH
REPEAT FROM HERE

IGNORE 'CODA' SIGN FIRST TIME THROUGH.
SECOND TIME THROUGH GO TO
CODA AT THE END OF THE MUSIC.

66

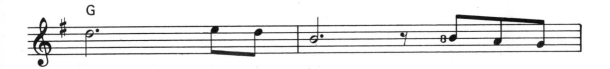

D.%. al Coda

GO BACK TO THE % SIGN AT THE BEGINNING
AND REPEAT THE MUSIC UNTIL YOU SEE 'TO CODA'

CODA

THIS COMES AT THE
END OF THE TUNE

An organ classic

This theme by Johann Sebastian Bach is one of the most famous organ solos of all time.

Classical music often sounds best if you play with the rhythm switched off, or with the rhythm volume turned down low. Try this music with the rhythm turned down low. For a short version of the music, go straight to the 'Coda' from the bottom of this page.

JESU, JOY OF MAN'S DESIRING

Organ (Add Stereo Chorus/Stereo Symphonic)
Waltz (Medium) (Add Variation/Arpeggio)

Music by JOHANN SEBASTIAN BACH
Adapted and Arranged by ROGER EVANS

REPEAT FROM HERE

SECOND TIME THROUGH GO TO 'CODA'
(FOR SHORT VERSION GO STRAIGHT TO CODA)

D.%. al Coda

REPEAT FROM % SIGN

⊕ *CODA*

Helpful hints and friendly advice

Have fun — play your keyboard with friends

You can have a lot of fun playing your keyboard with friends who play other instruments — or even another keyboard. At the same time, the extra practice will help your playing improve very quickly.

Playing with other instruments is not difficult — as long as you make sure you are in tune with each other before you begin.

If you are playing with a guitar, flute, recorder, violin and most other instruments, they should tune to your keyboard. If you play with another keyboard or organ you should already be in tune, but if you are not, one of you should adjust your pitch control.

If you want to play with B♭ instruments like the clarinet, trumpet or tenor saxophone *and read the same music,* you can do this if your keyboard has a 'transposer' and you set it to B♭, ♭2 or — 2. For E♭ instruments set the transposer to E♭, ♯3 or +3.

If you are playing with a piano — you should tune your keyboard to the piano. Do this by adjusting the pitch control on your keyboard until your Middle C sounds the same as the Middle C on the piano. (If you do not have a pitch control, or if it does not adjust far enough, try using the 'transposer' if your keyboard has one.)

Choose tunes which you and your friend both know well, and if possible read the same music. It is not a good idea to try anything new until you have had time to practise it on your own. If you do not know the same tunes, choose a piece of music together and practise it before you play together.

You will find that your keyboard blends well with most other instruments as long as you choose the right voices. Your auto bass chords and rhythm will also provide a good backing. However, if you play with another keyboard, only one of you should use auto rhythm as it is almost impossible to synchronise rhythms on two keyboards.

If you do not know anyone to play with, ask your local music shop if they know anyone or put an advertisement on a notice board or in a local paper. Do not be shy — many people will jump at the chance to have a keyboard player to play with.

Playing to an audience

Sooner or later someone is going to ask you to play for them. When this happens you should choose an easy tune which you can play confidently, almost without thinking about it. Please do not be tempted to play the most complicated tune you know, or the tune you have learned most recently as you are more likely to make mistakes with these.

Always take your time and think about the music you are going to play. Try to hear the tune in your head before you begin and adjust the rhythm to the right 'speed' by watching the tempo lamp on your keyboard as it flashes in time with the beat.

Never announce that "you cannot play very well" or "you will probably make mistakes" as this kind of talk will probably make you do these very things! If you do make a mistake, ignore it or make a joke of it — most people will probably not notice. Always remember that however little you play, you will be doing something that most other people cannot do and wish they could do — making music.

Playing for singing

Keyboards are really great for accompanying singing. The auto bass chords and rhythm section provide a full backing and keyboard voices blend well with singing. Why not sing along as you play your favourite songs and ask your family and friends to sing along with you at parties?

You can play melody, chords and rhythm together in the usual way to accompany singing. However, it can be very effective (and easier) to play just the chords and rhythm on their own as the backing for some songs. This allows you to concentrate on singing, and use your right hand to play solos and fill-ins between the verses of the song.

Once again, it is a good idea to try to hear the tune in your head before you begin and adjust the rhythm to the right speed by watching the tempo lamp flash with the beat.

Play the first note of the tune to give the singer a 'starting note' — or better still use the professional's trick of playing the first part or last part of the tune as an 'introduction' to lead the singer in.

If any songs are too high or too low for singing, use your transposer (if your keyboard has one) to adjust the pitch:

If the music is too high, try setting the transposer to B♭ (♭2 or —2) or G (♭5 or —5).

If the music is too low, set the transposer to E♭ (♯3 or +3) <u>or</u> F (♯5 or +5).

If your keyboard is easy to carry and can be powered by batteries you can enjoy yourself playing outside at picnics and parties, and even go carol singing with it.

If you play outside, make sure you have a waterproof cover for your keyboard in case it rains, and always take a spare set of batteries with you in case those in your keyboard fail. If you regularly play outside you will probably find it worth buying a set of rechargeable batteries which you can use again and again.

Playing by ear

Playing by ear is easier than you might think — as long as you do not try to play complicated music too soon. Like everything else, the secret is to learn to do it in easy stages.

Start with a tune you have already played, so you are playing partly from memory and partly by ear. It should be a tune you know well enough to sing or hum, but one which you could not play without reading the music. Anything will do, as long as it is short and simple, with no sharps or flats to complicate it. (Try any of the tunes in this book up to page 45, unless you remember them all completely.)

Read and play the first few notes to start you off, and sing or hum the whole tune several times until you are completely sure of it. Then, put the music away.

Now play the first few notes again and try to find the next note. If the melody goes up, try the next note higher than the last note you played. If this isn't high enough, try the next note higher still, and so on. If the melody seems to go down, try lower notes. Keep trying different notes (no sharps or flats for the moment) until you have the next note in the tune. Then look for the note which follows, and so on.

If you lose the tune, go back and play it again from the beginning to remind you. (It may help if you write down each note as you find it.) As long as you can manage to work out two or three notes by yourself, you are well on the way to playing by ear.

When you have worked out one tune, you will find other tunes easier, as long as you pick tunes you know very well, so you can tell when you are playing the right notes.

Chords and rhythms can also be worked out 'by ear'. Start by switching off the rhythm on your keyboard and play a C chord with your left thumb. (If you can't play chords on your keyboard with the rhythm switched off, choose a rhythm which suits the tune you are going to play and set the tempo much slower than usual.)

Keep your left thumb holding down the C chord key, so the C chord keeps sounding, and play the melody with the chord. (If you have trouble getting started, play the first few notes of the melody on their own to lead you in.) Keep playing the C chord and playing the melody, until the chord clashes with the melody. Then try other chords which you think might fit. (F, G, Am or Dm are the most likely.)

When you have found the right chord, play the tune from the beginning, changing to the second chord where it fits the tune. Continue playing with this chord until it too clashes with the melody. Then try other chords which you think might fit. (The third chord in the tune could be C again, or it could be one of the other chords suggested earlier.)

Then go on and work out the other chord changes in the same way.

If what you have worked out sounds right, it probably is right, but you can check by looking at the music if you are not sure.

When you are happy with the melody and chords, try playing the tune with different rhythms until you find one which suits the music best. Often several rhythms will seem almost as good, but choose whichever you think is right for the tune.

Next try an *easy* tune which you have not played, but which you know very well. (How about 'She'll Be Coming Round The Mountain When She Comes' or 'Happy Birthday To You'?)

First the melody. Play the C chord and try playing different notes with your right hand until you find the first note of the melody. (It will usually be C, E or G, although it could be any note played on the white keys.) Then find the next note, and the note after that, and so on.

(In case you find it hard to start, the first few notes of 'She'll Be Coming Round The Mountain When She Comes' are: G A C C C C A G E G C. The first notes of 'Happy Birthday To You' are: G G A G C B.)

When you have worked out the melody, try working out the chords and choose a rhythm as explained earlier. When you have done this, check the chords you have chosen by looking at the bottom of the page.

Try playing as many tunes as possible by ear, starting with short simple tunes to gain experience. (Even nursery rhymes or Christmas carols will do.) However, do not be disappointed if some do not work out straightaway — leave them to another day and try again.

Start with a C chord at first as this is easiest, and you will find you can play many tunes with C, F, and G chords, plus maybe Am, Dm or Em chords. Some tunes may also have other chords which you will need to find by trial and error. If a tune has a more sombre 'minor' chord feel about it, try starting with an A minor chord instead of a C chord. Later on you can try working out tunes starting with different chords. After some experience playing by ear and playing from music, you will begin to recognise the chord and melody patterns which fit most tunes.

Playing by ear is simply taking a tune which you can hear in your head, and finding the right notes and chords for it on your keyboard. As long as you can hear the notes in your head and have the patience to experiment and find the right notes and chords, you can work out many tunes. Playing by ear is not a substitute for reading music. Most musicians use both methods for learning new music.

The chords to 'She'll Be Coming Round The Mountain' go: C G C F C G C. The chords to 'Happy Birthday' go: C G C F C G C (with a Waltz rhythm.)

More advanced music

Here are some other notes and signs which you may find in modern music:

♬ is a SIXTEENTH NOTE. It usually lasts for a quarter of a beat.

Tap your foot and count sixteenth notes like this:

| 1 | 2 | 3 | 4 | 2 | 2 | 3 | 4 | 3 | 2 | 3 | 4 | 4 | 2 | 3 | 4 |

SIXTEENTH NOTES   SIXTEENTH NOTES WITH EIGHTH NOTES

A small '3' over a group of notes means they should be counted in three's:

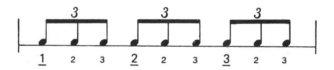

Try playing and counting all of these examples.

Sharps, Flats & Naturals

Remember, this is how sharps, flats and natural signs work:

Sharp (♯) or flat (♭) signs in the key signature affect *every note with the same name, all through the music.*

A sharp (♯), flat (♭) or natural sign (♮) in front of a note affects notes on the same line or space only up to the next bar-line.

74

More tunes for you to play

The small '3' over some of the notes in the next tune means they should be counted in three's. Play the melody on its own first, a little slower than usual. Tap your foot to the beat and follow the counting to get the timing of the notes right. As soon as you get the feeling of the melody, play the tune with chords and rhythm.

AMAZING GRACE

Violin/Strings
Waltz (Slow) (Add Variation/Arpeggio)

Adapted and Arranged
by ROGER EVANS

A pop music classic

This Mexican song has been a hit two or three times, and it became the theme music for a pop music movie.

The rhythm and chords start first to give the song an introduction. Count the beat so you know when to begin playing the melody.

LA BAMBA

Organ or Trumpet/Brass
Samba (Medium-Slow) (Add Variation/Arpeggio)

Adapted and Arranged
by ROGER EVANS

Scott Joplin's ragtime hit

The next tune started a ragtime music revival when it was used as the theme music for a film featuring Robert Redford and Paul Newman. Play it and have fun with it.

The tune is quite long, so learn it in two parts. The (7) and (Fm) chords are optional so you don't have to play them, but the music will sound better if you do.

THE ENTERTAINER

Piano/Guitar or Clarinet
March or Country (Medium)

Music by SCOTT JOPLIN
Adapted and Arranged by ROGER EVANS

FINISH SHORT
VERSION HERE

REPEAT FROM % SIGN

* New notes A♯ and B — see page 88.

A big band jazz classic

This jazz classic from the big band era sounds good played with the swing rhythm.

Take care — B♭ is in the key signature but there are also a few B natural notes in the music — and a G♯ which is played on the black key to the right of G. Follow the fingering carefully as you need to change fingers while you are playing some notes.

AMERICAN PATROL

Trumpet/Trombone or Jazz Organ
Swing (Medium-Fast)

Adapted and Arranged
by ROGER EVANS

(The last 4 bars have been repeated to finish.)

Playing Fingered Chords

When you play 'single finger chords', your keyboard automatically makes up chords for you by sounding three or four notes at the same time. It also makes up a bass pattern out of the notes of the chord. This works very well as long as the tunes you want to play can be played with the three or four different types of 'single finger chords' which most keyboards can produce. However, many tunes need more chords to be played effectively, and this is where the 'Fingered Chords' come in.

'Fingered Chords' give you a far wider selection of chords and enable more subtle backings to be played — while keeping all of the advantages of automatic bass lines and rhythms behind the melody. Learning to play fingered chords will improve your playing and help you to progress to jazz and some of the more advanced harmonies found in today's popular music.

Alright, let's set your keyboard to play some 'Fingered Chords':

1. Press or slide the auto bass chord selector to give 'Fingered Chords'.
2. Set the rhythm for 'Swing' or 'Slow Rock' (Medium). (You can use another rhythm if you like, but these give a good automatic bass line on most keyboards.)
3. Follow the fingering carefully, and rest your left hand lightly on the chord keys for the C chord shown here:

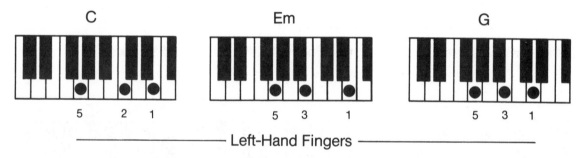

———————————— Left-Hand Fingers ————————————

4. When you are comfortable, press 'Synchro Start' with a right-hand finger. Then press your left hand down on the keys and listen to your 'fingered' C chord playing with the bass and rhythm.

Next, keep your little finger (5) on G, lift your index finger (2) off C and at the same time press down your middle finger (3) on B, and you're playing an E minor chord.

Now, move your thumb from E to D, and you are playing a G chord.

Finish with the C chord.

Relax, then play the chords again.

When you change chords, you can keep your fingers pressed down on any notes which are needed for the next chord. (This may not work if you use auto chord 'memory'.)

Let's play some more fingered chords. Follow the fingering very carefully, and keep your fingers on any keys which are needed for the next chord.

First find the C chord and press 'Synchro Start'. (The C chord is on the facing page.)

Now, lift your little finger (5) off G and at the same time press A with your ring finger (4) — and you are playing A minor:

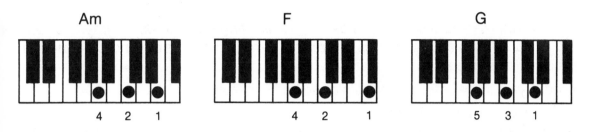

Next, move your thumb one key to the right to F, and you are playing an F chord.

Then, little finger (5) on G, middle finger (3) on B, and thumb on D to play a G chord.

Finally, keep your little finger on G, press C with your index finger (2) and E with your thumb, and you are playing a C chord again.

Let's try a few more fingered chords. Follow the fingering and try these:

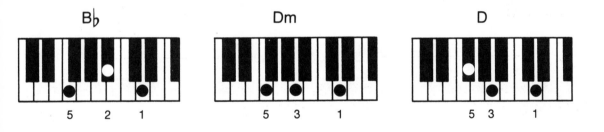

Now play this chord sequence two or three times with a Swing or Slow Rock rhythm:

Bb |Dm |D7 |G ||

The chords you have played here are all you need for most of the tunes in this book, so go back and play some of the tunes you know with 'fingered chords'.
Then come back and read the next page.

All of the fingered chords you have been playing so far could have been played in the 'single fingered chord' mode. Now we'll start to look at chords which cannot be played in the single fingered chord mode. Some of these chords have strange names, but they can be very important if you want to get the correct effect in many tunes.

Let's start with a chord called 'C major seventh'. This is usually written 'Cmaj7'. Follow the fingering shown here and play Cmaj7.

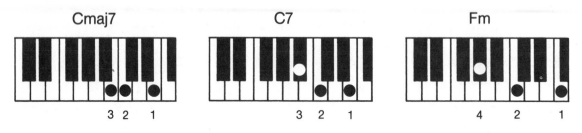

Now play the C7 chord shown here, and compare it with the Cmaj7 chord.

Next, play the F minor chord shown here, and compare it with an F chord.*

Relax a moment then play this chord sequence to see how these chords work together:*

Ballad/Pops (Medium)

C |Cmaj7 |C7 |F |Fm |C |G |C ||

Let's try another chord with an unusual name — 'C augmented'. This is usually written 'C+' or 'C aug':

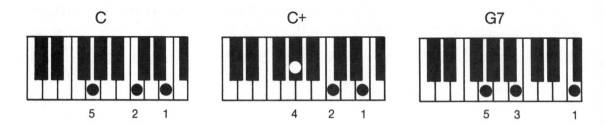

Play a C chord, then the C+ chord. Also try changing from a C chord to the G7 chord and back again to C. Then, when you are ready, play this chord sequence. It will give you some good practice playing fingered chords*:

Ballad/Pops (Medium)

C |C+ |Am |C7 |F |G7 |C ||

*Look up the C, F, G and Am chords on the previous pages if you are unsure about them.

Going on from here

Congratulations! After playing your way through this book you have gained a lot of experience as a keyboard player, and you are on your way to becoming a good musician.

In these pages you have played many different types of music — popular music, classical music, jazz, Latin American music and music from the sunny islands of the Caribbean.

Now you can make your own choice, and decide whether you want to continue playing a broad variety of different types of music, or concentrate on one particular kind. Whatever you decide, follow the advice given on the next page on learning to play new music.

You have played music with many different voices and rhythms in this book, plus some interesting keyboard effects, but we probably still haven't explored all of the features of your keyboard. If you still haven't tried all of the voices, rhythms or special effects on your keyboard, you should try them now. Simply remember to choose voices, rhythms or effects which suit the music you are playing. Also be sure you do not over-use any particular voice, rhythm or effect, or your music could start to sound too much the same.

Now would also be a good time to go back over anything you found at all difficult and try it again. You will probably find everything is easier now you have left it for a while. In fact if you ever find anything difficult it often helps to leave it and come back to it later. I often leave difficult things overnight and come back to them the next day when they usually seem far easier.

For the future always try to play as well as possible, and avoid getting into bad habits. If you are ever unsure of anything you learned here, come back to this book and read about it again.

I hope you have enjoyed all of the music in this book. In the next pages there is advice to help you to choose your own music, a 'keyboard note finder' where you can look up any notes which you may not remember, plus a good selection of 'fingered chords' for every key.

Here's wishing you a lot of fun playing your keyboard.

Learning to play new music

Now you are ready to broaden your horizons by choosing your own music to play.

The easiest way to learn to play new tunes is to buy printed music for tunes you like. Look for books of 'easy keyboard music' in your local music shop, and choose books which include tunes you know well.

Start with short, easy tunes, and avoid music with more than one or two sharps or flats in the key signature at first.

As an ideal follow-on to this book, I recommend my *Playing Keyboards* easy music books, which are perfect for your level of playing. Every *Playing Keyboards* book features special easy keyboard arrangements of well-known tunes, all in the same easy style as the music you have played in this book. The *Playing Keyboards* tutor book gives playing hints, advice, and some good tunes to play. *Playing Keyboards* songbooks feature hit songs and popular music, TV and film themes, Christmas songs and carols, classical hits and more. *(Playing Keyboards* books are obtainable from all good music shops and by mail order from Express Music, PO Box 153, London WC2H 0EA.)

Whatever music you choose, learn to play each new tune in easy stages. If you like you can play the melody and chords separately before you put them together with the rhythm.

Before you begin, look through the music to make sure you know how to play all of the notes and chords, and look up any you may have forgotten.

See which sharps or flats are in the key signature, and remember they affect *every* note with the same name. Work out how you are going to move your fingers smoothly from one note to the next, before you worry about the timing of the notes.

Play through the chords and make sure you can change smoothly from each chord to the next chord.

Play the tune slowly and evenly at first, then gradually work up to the correct speed. Practise any awkward parts on their own until you have mastered them.

If the music does not sound right when you play it, check you are reading the music correctly and following every sharp, flat and natural sign. Refer to this book if you are unsure of anything you learned here.

Always learn to play each piece of music correctly and smoothly before going on to something new, or you may end up knowing how to play parts of lots of tunes without being able to play any of them correctly.

Also see 'How to read sheet music' on the next page if you want to play music from 'piano/vocal' books or sheet music.

How to read sheet music

Some music you want to play may not be available in 'easy keyboard' books. In this case you should look for books of 'piano/vocal' music, standard 'sheet music', or even music for other instruments like the guitar. As long as the music has chord symbols and the melody on the 'top line', you should be able to read it. A typical piece of piano/vocal sheet music looks like this, with the melody shown over the piano part:

CHORD SYMBOL (Chord name)

GUITAR CHORDS

THE 'TOP LINE' — FOR MELODY PLAYING AND SINGING. (This is what you play with your right hand.)
1st TIME LYRICS
2nd TIME LYRICS

THE PIANO PART.

(The 𝄞 stave is for the right hand. The 𝄢 stave is for the left hand.)

You can read and play the 'top line' and chords in the same way as the music you have played in this book. Of course, you may need to decide for yourself which voices and rhythms to use. This is no real problem — simply play the tune with different voices and rhythms until you find voices and rhythms which suit the music.

The piano part in sheet music is usually a piano solo. As you can see, a separate stave is used for the right hand and left hand on the piano. The left hand usually plays the accompaniment including bass notes and chords; while the right hand usually plays the melody, sometimes also with chords.

You can use most keyboards as a piano, and play piano music on them (preferably using a 'piano' or 'electric piano' voice), if you set the auto bass chord section to 'normal' or 'off'. Of course, you will need to know how to play like a pianist and learn to read music written with the 𝄢 clef. If you would like to do this please see my book *How To Play Piano,* which is in the same series as this book and published by Elm Tree Books in association with EMI Music Publishing.

Keyboard note-finder

You can use this page to look up melody notes when you are learning to play new music.

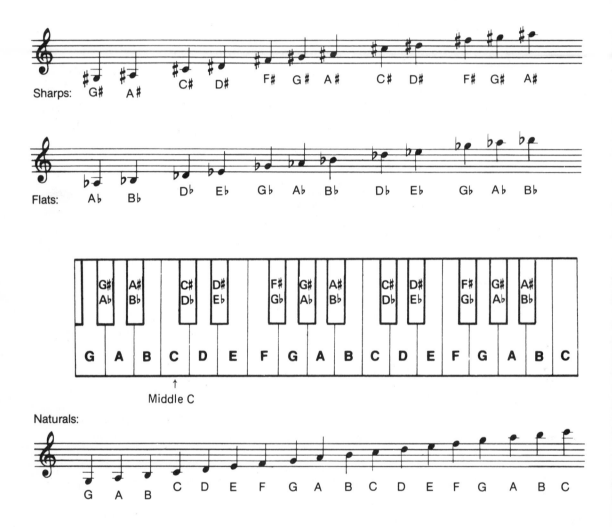

Sharps: G# A# C# D# F# G# A# C# D# F# G# A#

Flats: Ab Bb Db Eb Gb Ab Bb Db Eb Gb Ab Bb

Middle C

Naturals: G A B C D E F G A B C D E F G A B C

Fingered chords for every key

In the following pages you will find fingered chords for every key — C, Cm, C♯, C♯m and so on. You do not need to learn all of these chords right away, because you can look them up whenever you come across them in music. However, it would be a good idea to play through all of the chords for the more usual keys — C, F, B♭, G, and D, as well as the A minor and E minor chords.

You will find some more chords with unusual names in the next pages:

'C°' or 'C dim' means this chord is a 'C diminished' chord. On their own diminished chords sound as though they should be part of a silent movie or a horror show, but they are also often mixed with other chords. Play C♯° (C sharp diminished), then play the chord sequence which follows to see how a diminished chord is often used. (If you cannot remember all of the chords, look them up in the next few pages.)

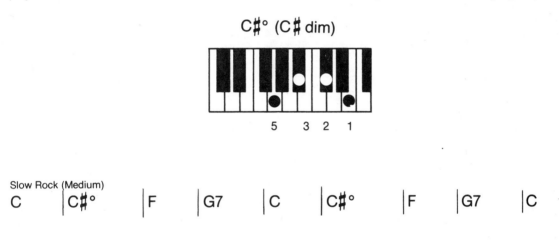

C♯° (C♯ dim)

Slow Rock (Medium)

| C | C♯° | F | G7 | C | C♯° | F | G7 | C |

'C7sus4' is another chord with an unusual name. You can usually play an ordinary seventh chord instead of '7sus4' chords, but the effect may not be as good.

Another strange chord is 'Cm7-5'. This is 'C minor seventh minus 5', sometimes written 'Cm7♭5'. Go to the next page, and compare Cm7-5 with Cm, Cm7 and C°.

The chords shown in these pages have been selected because they work well with the auto chord sections on most keyboards. There are other chords which do not work as well, or which cannot be played correctly as 'fingered chords', and I have suggested chords which can be played instead of these at the bottom of each page.

For more advanced playing, you could buy a book of chords from your music dealer and play any chord you wish. To do this you should set your keyboard's auto chord selector to 'normal' or 'off'. You will then be able to play any chord with an automatic rhythm, although you will lose the benefits of automatic bass notes with your chords.

C chords

C
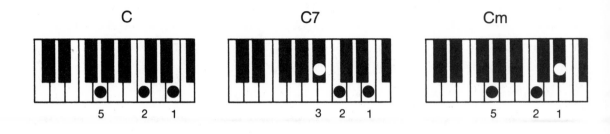

5 2 1

C7

3 2 1

Cm

5 2 1

Cmaj7
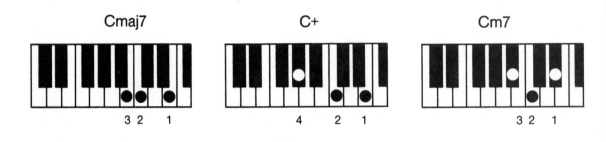

3 2 1

C+

4 2 1

Cm7

3 2 1

C°
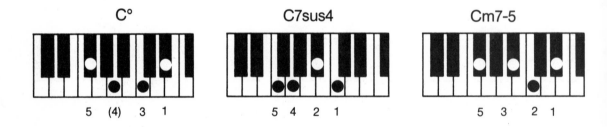

5 (4) 3 1

C7sus4

5 4 2 1

Cm7-5

5 3 2 1

Other C chords:

You can play a C chord instead of these chords: C6; C6/9; Csus; Csus4

You can play a C7 chord instead of these chords: C7-9; C7+9; C7-5; C9; C11; C13

You can play a Cm chord instead of these chords: Cm6; Cm6/9; Cmsus; Cmsus4

You can play a Cm7 chord instead of these chords: Cm7sus4; Cm9; Cm11

C♯ and D♭ chords

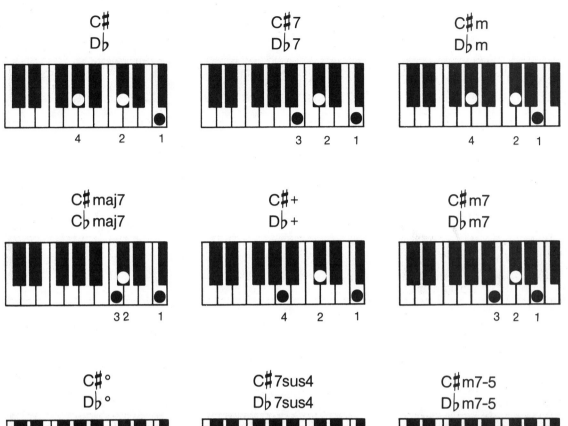

C♯
D♭

C♯7
D♭7

C♯m
D♭m

4 2 1

3 2 1

4 2 1

C♯maj7
C♭maj7

C♯+
D♭+

C♯m7
D♭m7

3 2 1

4 2 1

3 2 1

C♯°
D♭°

C♯7sus4
D♭7sus4

C♯m7-5
D♭m7-5

5 (3) 2 1

5 4 2 1

5 3 2 1

Other C♯ and D♭ chords:

You can play a C♯/D♭ chord instead of these chords: C♯/D♭6; C♯/D♭6/9; C♯/D♭sus; C♯/D♭sus4

You can play a C♯/D♭7 chord instead of these chords: C♯/D♭7-9; C♯/D♭7+9; C♯/D♭7-5; C♯/D♭9; C♯/D♭11; C♯/D♭13

You can play a C♯/D♭m chord instead of these chords: C♯/D♭m6; C♯/D♭m6/9; C♯/D♭msus; D♭/D♭msus4

You can play a C♯/D♭m7 chord instead of these chords: Cm♯/D♭7sus4; C♯/D♭m9; C♯/D♭m11

D chords

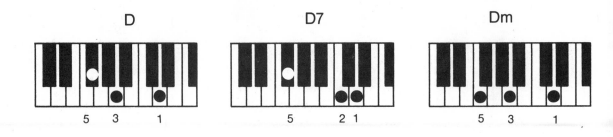

D	D7	Dm
5 3 1	5 2 1	5 3 1

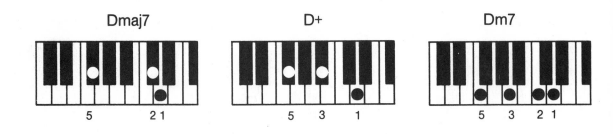

Dmaj7	D+	Dm7
5 2 1	5 3 1	5 3 2 1

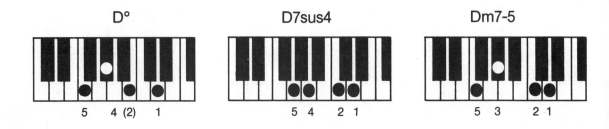

D°	D7sus4	Dm7-5
5 4 (2) 1	5 4 2 1	5 3 2 1

Other D chords:

You can play a D chord instead of these chords: D6; D6/9; Dsus; Dsus4

You can play a D7 chord instead of these chords: D7-9; D7+9; D7-5; D9; D11; D13

You can play a Dm chord instead of these chords: Dm6; Dm6/9; Dmsus; Dmsus4

You can play a Dm7 chord instead of these chords: Dm7sus4; Dm9; Dm11

E♭ (and D♯) chords

E♭
(D♯)

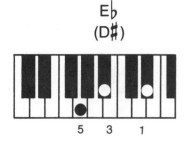

5 3 1

E♭7
(D♯7)

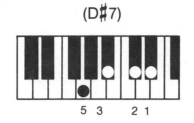

5 3 2 1

E♭m
(D♯m)

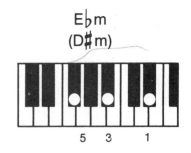

5 3 1

E♭maj7
(D♯maj7)

5 3 2 1

E♭+
(D♯+)

5 3 1

E♭m7
(D♯m7)

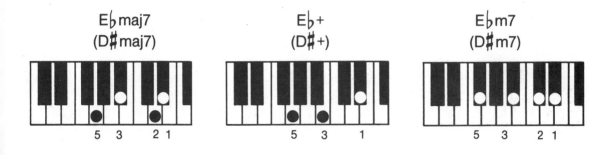

5 3 2 1

E♭°
(D♯°)

5 4 2 1

E♭7sus4
(D♯7sus4)

5 4 2 1

E♭m7-5
(D♯m7-5)

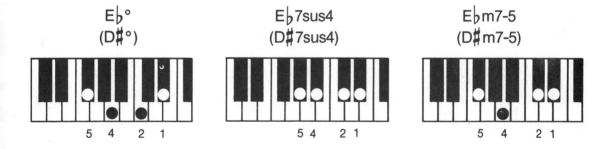

5 4 2 1

Other E♭ (and D♯) chords:

You can play an E♭/D♯ chord instead of these chords: E♭/D♯6; E♭/D♯6/9; E♭/D♯sus; E♭/D♯sus4

You can play a E♭/D♯7 chord instead of these chords: E♭/D♯7-9; E♭/D♯7+9; E♭/D♯7-5; E♭/D♯9; E♭/D♯11; E♭/D♯13

You can play a E♭/D♯m chord instead of these chords: E♭/D♯m6; E♭/D♯m6/9; E♭/D♯msus; E♭/D♯msus4

You can play a E♭/D♯m7 chord instead of these chords: E♭/D♯m7sus4; E♭/D♯m9; E♭/D♯m11

E chords

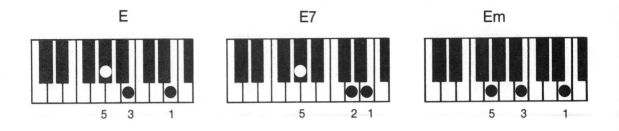

E   5 3 1

E7   5   2 1

Em   5 3 1

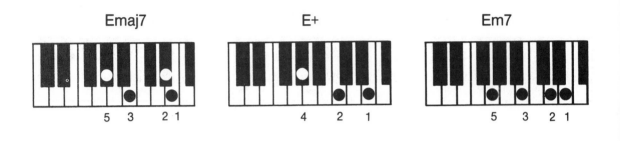

Emaj7 5 3 2 1

E+   4 2 1

Em7 5 3 2 1

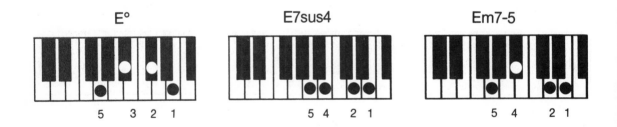

E°   5 3 2 1

E7sus4 5 4 2 1

Em7-5 5 4 2 1

Other E chords:

You can play an E chord instead of these chords: E6; E6/9; Esus; Esus4

You can play an E7 chord instead of these chords: E7-9; E7+9; E7-5; E9; E11; E13

You can play an Em chord instead of these chords: Em6; Em6/9; Emsus; Emsus4

You can play an Em7 chord instead of these chords: Em7sus4; Em9; Em11

F chords

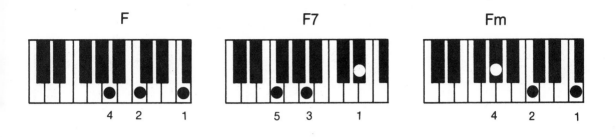

F	F7	Fm
4 2 1	5 3 1	4 2 1

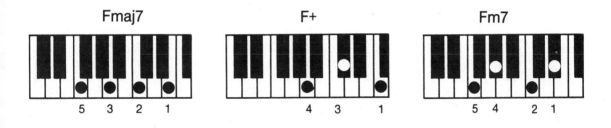

Fmaj7	F+	Fm7
5 3 2 1	4 3 1	5 4 2 1

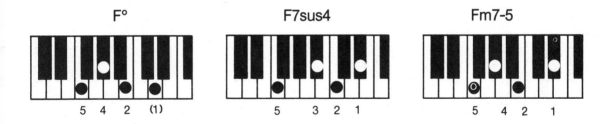

F°	F7sus4	Fm7-5
5 4 2 (1)	5 3 2 1	5 4 2 1

Other F chords:

You can play an F chord instead of these chords: F6; F6/9; Fsus; Fsus4

You can play an F7 chord instead of these chords: F7-9; F7+9; F7-5; F9; F11; F13

You can play an Fm chord instead of these chords: Fm6; Fm6/9; Fmsus; Fmsus4

You can play an Fm7 chord instead of these chords: Fm7sus4; Fm9; Fm11

F♯ and G♭ chords

F♯
G♭
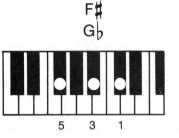

5 3 1

F♯7
G♭7
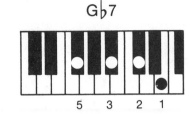

5 3 2 1

F♯m
G♭m
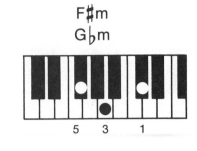

5 3 1

F♯maj7
G♭maj7

5 4 2

F♯+
G♭+

5 3 1

F♯m7
G♭m7

5 4 2 1

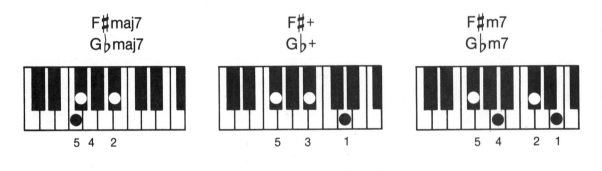

F♯°
G♭°
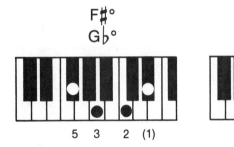

5 3 2 (1)

F♯7sus4
G♭7sus4
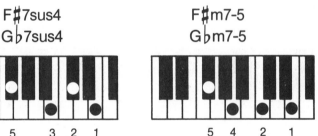

5 3 2 1

F♯m7-5
G♭m7-5

5 4 2 1

Other F♯ and G♭ chords:

You can play an F♯/G♭ chord instead of these chords: F♯/G♭6; F♯G♭6/9; F♯/G♭sus; F♯/G♭sus4

You can play an F♯/G♭7 chord instead of these chords: F♯/G♭7-9; F♯/G♭7+9; F♯/G♭7-5; F♯/G♭9; F♯/G♭11; F♯/G♭13

You can play an F♯/G♭m chord instead of these chords: F♯/G♭m6; F♯/G♭m6/9; F♯/G♭m9; F♯/G♭msus; F♯/G♭msus4

You can play an F♯/G♭m7 chord instead of these chords: F♯/G♭m7sus4; F♯/G♭m9; F♯/G♭m11

G chords

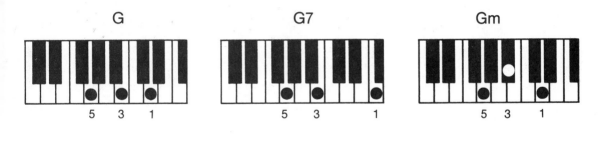

G   5 3 1

G7   5 3 1

Gm   5 3 1

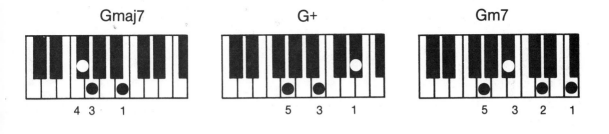

Gmaj7   4 3 1

G+   5 3 1

Gm7   5 3 2 1

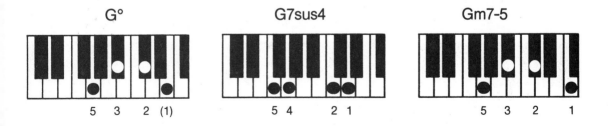

G°   5 3 2 (1)

G7sus4   5 4 2 1

Gm7-5   5 3 2 1

Other G chords:

You can play a G chord instead of these chords: G6; G6/9; Gsus; Gsus4

You can play a G7 chord instead of these chords: G7-9; G7+9; G7-5; G9; G11; G13

You can play a Gm chord instead of these chords: Gm6; Gm6/9; Gmsus; Gmsus4

You can play a Gm7 chord instead of these chords: Gm7sus4; Gm9; Gm11

A♭ (and G♯) chords

A♭
(G♯)

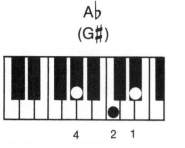

4 2 1

A♭7
(G♯7)

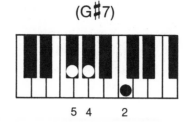

5 4   2

A♭m
(G♯m)

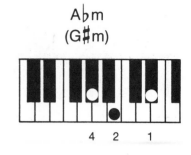

4   2   1

A♭maj7
(G♯maj7)

5 4 2

A♭+
(G♯+)

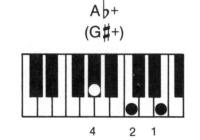

4   2 1

A♭m7
(G♯m7)

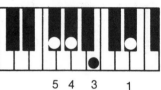

5 4 3   1

A♭°
(G♯°)

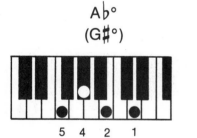

5 4 2 1

A♭7sus4
(G♯7sus4)

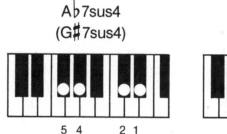

5 4   2 1

A♭m7-5
(G♯m7-5)

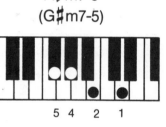

5 4 2 1

Other A♭ (and G♯) chords:

You can play an A♭/G♯ chord instead of these chords: A♭/G♯6; A♭/G♯6/9; A♭/G♯sus; A♭/G♯sus4

You can play an A♭/G♯7 chord instead of these chords: A♭/G♯7-9; A♭/G♯7+9; A♭/G♯7-5; A♭/G♯9; A♭/G♯11; A♭/G♯13

You can play an A♭/G♯m chord instead of these chords: A♭/G♯m6; A♭/G♯m6/9; A♭/G♯msus; A♭/G♯msus4

You can play an A♭/G♯m7 chord instead of these chords: A♭/G♯m7sus4; A♭/G♯m9; A♭/G♯m11

A chords

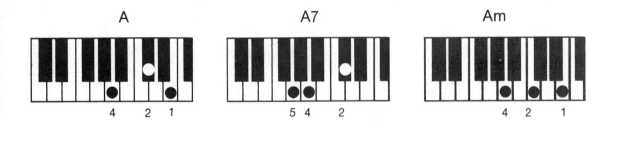

A   4 2 1

A7   5 4 2

Am   4 2 1

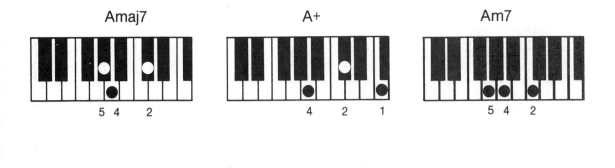

Amaj7   5 4 2

A+   4 2 1

Am7   5 4 2

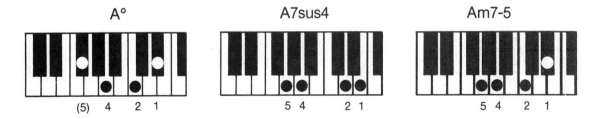

A°   (5) 4 2 1

A7sus4   5 4   2 1

Am7-5   5 4 2 1

Other A chords:

You can play an A chord instead of these chords: A6; A6/9; Asus; Asus4

You can play an A7 chord instead of these chords: A7-9; A7+9; A7-5; A9; A11; A13

You can play an Am chord instead of these chords: Am6; Am6/9; Amsus; Amsus4

You can play an Am7 chord instead of these chords: Am7sus4; Am9; Am11

B♭ (and A♯) chords

B♭
(A♯)

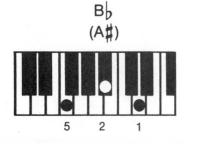

5   2   1

B♭7
(A♯7)

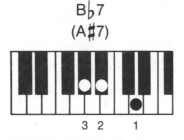

3   2   1

B♭m
(A♯m)

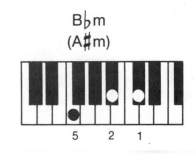

5   2   1

B♭maj7
(A♯maj7)

3 2   1

B♭+
(A♯+)

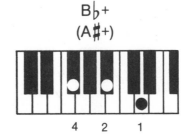

4   2   1

B♭m7
(A♯m7)

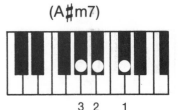

3   2   1

B♭°
(A♯°)

5   3   2   1

B♭7sus4
(A♯7sus4)

(5)   3   2   1

B♭m7-5
(A♯m7-5)

4   3   2   1

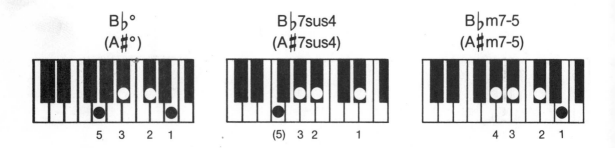

Other B♭ (and A♯) chords:

You can play a B♭/A♯ chord instead of these chords: B♭/A♯6; B♭/A♯6/9; B♭/A♯sus; B♭/A♯sus4

You can play a B♭/A♯7 chord instead of these chords: B♭/A♯7-9; B♭/A♯7+9; B♭/A♯7-5; B♭/A♯9; B♭/A♯11; B♭/A♯13

You can play a B♭/A♯m chord instead of these chords: B♭/A♯m6; B♭/A♯m6/9; B♭/A♯msus; B♭/A♯msus4

You can play a B♭/A♯m7 chord instead of these chords: B♭/A♯m7sus4; B♭/A♯m9; B♭/A♯m11

B chords

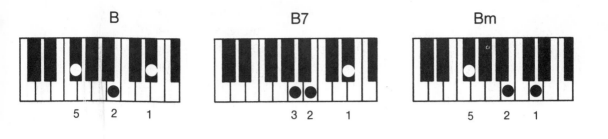

B   5   2   1

B7   3   2   1

Bm   5   2   1

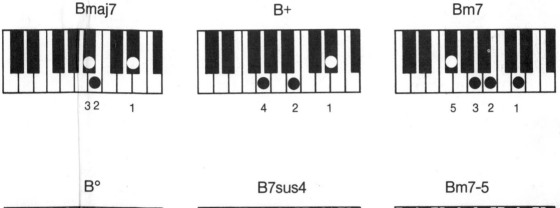

Bmaj7   3   2   1

B+   4   2   1

Bm7   5   3   2   1

B°   5   (4)   2   1

B7sus4   (5)   3   2   1

Bm7-5   5   3   2   1

Other B chords:

You can play a B chord instead of these chords: B6; B6/9; Bsus; Bsus4

You can play a B7 chord instead of these chords: B7-9; B7+9; B7-5; B9; B11; B13

You can play a Bm chord instead of these chords: Bm6; Bm6/9; Bmsus; Bmsus4

You can play a Bm7 chord instead of these chords: Bm7sus4; Bm9; Bm11

Index

Music in this book